A MODERN FRENCH REPUBLIC

Also by Pierre Mendès France

THE PURSUIT OF FREEDOM
Longmans, Green and Co. (London, 1956)

Written with Gabriel Ardant

ECONOMICS AND ACTION
Columbia University Press (New York, 1955)

A MODERN FRENCH REPUBLIC

PIERRE MENDÈS FRANCE

Translated by
ANNE CARTER

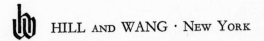 HILL AND WANG · NEW YORK

In memory of Georges Boris
an irreplaceable friend
P.M.F.

CONTENTS

PREFACE TO
THE AMERICAN EDITION

THIS BOOK was written with a French audience in mind, and it is particularly concerned with the problems which France is facing at the present time.

Nevertheless, I am delighted to know that it is to be published in America – as it has been, or soon will be, in a number of other countries – because the questions raised in it affect democratically minded people everywhere where there is a rapidly expanding economy creating a very different frame from that of the nineteenth century. This is especially true of those affluent societies which have been the subject of so many reflections and studies in America.

Naturally the problems dealt with in this book will present themselves in very different terms in the United States or Canada from those which apply in western Europe, and France in particular. But we all face the need for a fresh attitude to the problem of reconciling the ideals of freedom and democracy with an efficiently-run State.

The way in which political institutions should be related to organised economic and social forces; methods by which political organisations can deal with economic affairs formerly outside their jurisdiction; the representation of and the degree of personal intervention by the ordinary citizen who is also a producer, a worker, a consumer: nowadays these preoccupations belong equally to all people, in all countries, who

A*   9 are trying to find the best conditions for the workings of a modern State.

Moreover, anything which happens in Europe or North America has inevitable repercussions on the other side of the Atlantic, both from an economic point of view and from that of the general social and political climate. We can no longer pursue our own development schemes and our economic, monetary and trade policies in isolation as we did in the past. The arguments and negotiations which proceed within the OECD, GATT and European organisations offer daily proof of this.

To an increasing extent our decisions will have been brought into line with one another, and carried out in conjunction. For all these reasons we must get to know and understand one another better and better, so that each may be more fully aware of what his partners are doing. If, as I hope and believe, this book provides a faithful picture of the aspirations of a certain number of young French people, it may well be of some use to those of our friends on the other side of the Atlantic who are interested in knowing what goes on in Europe.

Frontiers and oceans should not prove a barrier to discussion of the part to be played by the individual in a city whose primary aims are freedom, consistency and progress, and of the way in which he can best play his part in the life of the community. This is the main consideration which has led me to submit these views to those Americans who are concerned, as many of us in France are, with building a truly Modern Democracy.

Pierre Mendès France
Paris, May, 1963

FOREWORD

WHAT ARE the conditions governing our institutions in the second half of the twentieth century, and what should be their aims? This is the question I am attempting to answer in this book, bearing in mind the economic, social and psychological structure of a nation such as France at this point in her history.

If we hope to see one kind of solution to the problem accepted rather than another, then we must make these solutions clear in advance. We must know that they have been considered, argued, rejected, perhaps, by some and accepted with reservations by others or accepted unconditionally by others again. The ideal situation would be for every individual citizen to choose for himself. It is not important whether my proposals are criticised here and there, what matters is that they exist. Once they provoke discussion they are doing their job and contributing to the revival of political life and preparation for the future. Then, whenever the problem of the new régime has to be faced, French public opinion will be ready with its decision.

The following essay lays no claim to originality: many of the ideas outlined in it have been argued out in very different parties and environments. What we have to do is to arrive at the greatest common denominator of all that has been accepted by all sides. This common denominator is in itself an important basis for uniting men who are now very far apart. It should

11

make it possible for them to work out a political agreement which all the forces of progress may one day join in putting into practice.

This is no intangible basis of agreement. It may leave room for improvement and finishing in method and detail; but it provides a whole in which each part is connected with the rest. For instance there is little point in rebuilding the best political institutions unless they are linked to the machinery of a democratic economy; and reorganising the Second Chamber of Parliament so that today's social and economic facts are represented would do more harm than good if, at the same time, the National Assembly was denied effective means of exercising political control in the name of the sovereign people. There would be no sense in organised economic planning unless we first defined for whom and for what we are planning, unless we provided the means to make our planning effective, unless it was developed, carried out and supervised by qualified professional and social organisations, and unless the government could be expected, at least as a general rule, to last as long as the plan itself.

Nevertheless, this basis of agreement is only a minimum, since each one of the reforms under consideration will bear fruit only if the others are also accepted; and if it is understood that once a particular object has been decided upon, everything should be done to achieve it.

My immediate answer to anyone who complains that I have left some important questions out of this book is that it was not my intention to draw up a catalogue of desirable reforms. Such catalogues do exist, we have seen them all too often, but a multiplicity of promises has never been a guarantee of results. Provisional and incomplete proposals which are honestly in line with possibilities are worth more than sweeping but misused publicity.

I would add, too, that as a whole, the proposals set out here claim priority over further developments. I defy any French politician or political party whatsoever to set about an immediate and authentic democratisation of education, to adjust the distribution of the nation's income in favour of the under-privileged classes, to ensure that state control will have a dominant position in the economy, to enforce a new respect for the fundamental liberties and rights of man, and to command the obedience of an army which is at one with the nation as a whole—unless they have first provided a proper solution to these institutional problems. In other words, unless they have chosen the right tools for the job.

We shall have made a great step forward when the bulk of the men and women in this country become fully aware of the situation and the responsibilities which arise from it.

In 1789, the French peasantry and bourgeoisie knew what they wanted: land and the abolition of privilege. In 1917, the workers and peasants of Russia knew what they wanted: peace, land and food. Today, France has no such simple, desperate hunger, although the demands of her situation were fundamentally just as serious. She must start a new and hitherto untried experiment: the setting up of a democracy which is simultaneously political and economic within a great, modern nation. Intelligence and understanding must therefore replace an obvious necessity.

Political development depends on economic and social structures. But these structures are never absolutely stable or absolutely homogeneous. They contain variable and changing combinations of divergent pressures which clash, or of convergent pressures which come together. This country is like a super-cooled liquid, giving no indication of the surprising potentialities that might suddenly be revealed in the smallest particle; one day it might demand sweeping reforms. Is it not already living in expectation of them?

We must be ready for whatever happens. We must forestall the event, and define and clarify our ideas of the direction we wish our country to take*.

---

* I should like to thank Colette Audry for her perceptive and devoted help in the preparation of this book.

13

PART ONE

THE FACTS

CHAPTER ONE

DOUBTS AND CONVICTIONS
OF FRENCHMEN

I HAVE travelled a great deal, in the past year*, through urban
and rural districts of France. My travels were more than a
matter of simply rushing from one big town to the next,
appearing one evening and leaving again first thing the following morning. The meetings I held were never my main object.
I went primarily in order to meet people—individually and in
small groups—whose jobs and interests kept them abreast of
affairs in their own regions and the affairs of the nation at large.

I talked to the directors of big companies and the heads of
professional and cultural organisations, to trades union officials
and representatives of workers and management in both
industry and agriculture, and to members of student bodies.
I talked to them in their official and private capacities, but all
of them, whether they were artisans, graduates, doctors,
magistrates, journalists, civil servants or politicians, left or
right wing, politically committed or uninterested and hostile to
politics, had one thing in common: they were in close touch
with the real life of the nation and all felt to some extent
responsible for its future development.

I went from Grenoble to Lille, from Rennes to Clermont-
Ferrand, from Bordeaux to Strasbourg, listening to their
opinions, criticisms and forecasts. They told me about their

---

* 1961-1962.

fears and anxieties. I am grateful to them for helping me to a better understanding of present day France.

There are bound to be complaints that interviews of this kind invariably fail to take account of the vast bulk of the population who, while deeply concerned with events, do not feel they are in any way committed. These are the people who might be described as the 'silent nation' in contrast to that part of the nation which expresses its views through debate, articles and statements. They form the crowds who line the route when the head of state goes by and then vanish into obscurity again: but it is they who, once roused, or even by the simple act of placing their vote in the ballot box, decide who is to govern.

In fact, the complex network of individuals to whom I talked is in no way cut off from the deeper levels of society: it is immersed in it. Each spokesman for a particular group keeps a continual watch on the climate of public opinion. People sometimes point out that only a fifth of the working population belongs to a union, but whenever the major unions take concerted action they are followed by the whole of a particular trade, and sometimes by the entire working class.

The spectator should not be led astray by the cheering crowds which greet the President's public appearances. They fulfil the popular love of spectacle and express a certain transitory state of feeling, but there are, in fact, no long or short term conclusions about the future to be drawn from them. This state of mind can fluctuate from one day to the next.

I have accumulated my evidence over a period of many months full of political upheavals in France and of violent feelings. When an investigation reveals, as it does in this case, several major points of agreement, and when these emerge at the outset and remain constant throughout a period of such intense activity, it is fair to conclude that they represent a deeply-rooted public belief. The nation should be made aware of this, since it is this realisation which shapes the outline of the future course of events. Once this happens, one can say that the events have already begun: they are already a political fact.

18

The Points of Agreement

What are these points of agreement?

1 It is common knowledge that the régime we have been living under since 1958 is only an interim situation. Many of the men I spoke to voted *oui* in the various referendums and have not regretted doing so; there were also those who voted *non*. None, however, believes that the Fifth Republic can survive. The most optimistic assume that 'the present system will last as long as de Gaulle does'. Even they are already facing the problem of what will happen afterwards.

2 Public opinion is widely felt to be vague and apathetic. The truth is that the people are waiting; and waiting is an uncomfortable state (and has nothing to do with indifference), so they are trying to forget the fact. They are suffering from a kind of paralysis in the face of an uncertain future.

For the first time in a long while, Frenchmen felt the threat of civil war and were frightened. Consequently, many are inclined to prolong the breathing space afforded by de Gaulle's leadership. Yet at the same time they are anxious about what has become known as 'the void'.

It is this void which the men who planted plastic bombs were (and still are) claiming to fill. Stock piling of weapons; the unreliability of a number of army officers, and even of whole units; and the way in which the extremists, whose aims are as clear-cut as ever, are exploiting the bitterness and resentment of countless French Algerian refugees: all these are well known facts. The extremists may be prevented from reaching their goals, but they are still capable of creating a sufficiently tense situation for the army chiefs to intervene on the pretext of 'arbitration', or for another so-called national union to be proposed as a cloak for one, all-powerful faction which would gradually lead the country into fascism.

The vast bulk of the country is deeply hostile to the pressures of the extreme right and the terrorists. The French people are revolted by their use of torture, and their, by now notorious, contempt for civil and individual liberties and human dignity.

19

A succession of plastic bomb outrages, kidnappings and murders carried out in Paris itself have shown that these methods are not confined to the opposite shores of the Mediterranean and that, far from being merely the dying convulsions of an obsolete colonial system, they represent a direct threat to France and a grave foretaste of the future. Many people may be intimidated by them, but this does not alter the fact that Frenchmen react with horror against the very idea of a fascist or a police state. Even those who do not believe there is any immediate danger would be apprehensive should de Gaulle be removed from power for any reason. Once more the question arises: what would happen then?

I have plenty of evidence to show that Frenchmen are intensely preoccupied by any attempt to see into and prepare for the future from that point onwards. Moreover here too there are clearly broad areas of agreement.

3 In the first place, no one wants to see a return to the Fourth Republic, which remains in everyone's mind as the picture of impotence in every respect: incapable alike of original ideas, decision, authority and constructive action; a régime of cabals, perpetual instability and weakness in the face of every kind of pressure.

It might have been thought that the end of the war in Algeria, marking for all practical purposes the end of a programme of retreat from the colonial system, would have been a signal for what some experts call 'a return to normal'. Ever since the outbreak of war in Indo-China the Fourth Republic had been rocked by the convulsions arising from this process, and there are still some people who attribute the Republic's fall to an apparent incapacity to ensure that it happened smoothly, rather than to an inefficient and muddle-headed conception of democracy*. This being so, once the reason for the

---

* In actual fact the Algerian war demonstrated with blinding clarity that *as far as doing away with the colonial system was concerned* the Fourth Republic functioned in such a way as effectively to prevent any government from solving the country's problems. It certainly provided a terrible warning—but that was all.

20

disorder had been removed, what were the objections to reverting to the former system?

In any event, this 'return to normal' will never come about because the country refuses to consider the Fourth Republic as normal. Recent statements by Maurice Thorez, General Secretary of the French Communist party, show that even the Communists are aware of having committed a serious blunder in calling for the *restoration* of democracy. The word implied all too clearly the very things which no one wanted to see restored.

I made several attempts to demonstrate, during the Fourth Republic, that our institutions and, to an even greater extent, habits, paralysed any government which wanted to act upon major issues. This the men in power failed to realise, while the people became aware of it only very slowly and offered no support to those who were trying to improve the situation. This time, however, the facts are obvious and can be taken for granted.

4 But being against the Fourth Republic does not necessarily mean a wish to see a régime where power is concentrated indefinitely in the hands of one man. Even those who entrusted General de Gaulle with unlimited authority did not for a moment envisage handing the same authority to his successor. De Gaulle owes his present position to three things: his past, his age (he showed himself fully aware of this in 1958 when he remarked: 'I am sixty-nine. A man does not court dictatorships at my age'.), and the fact that he was considered to be a man of exceptional character, capable of ruling in exceptional circumstances.

I have already pointed out that most people feel that France has been going through an intermediary phase since 1958 (although opinions differ about whether or not this was necessary). No one believes this interlude can last. It is the exception, not the rule.

The Transition

The country is perfectly clear about what it does *not* want: there must be no parliamentary government of the kind already experienced, and no acceptance of the idea of personal power as a permanent way of life.

But beyond these points there is no certainty, and any ideas that may be discussed come up against a barrier of cynicism, evasiveness or profound distrust. This can be seen from the depressing phrases which crop up continually, like a refrain, on all sides: there is no alternative, there *ought* to be another way out . . . As long as there is no other solution de Gaulle will stay in power . . . and so on. These are things people say when they feel that circumstances have gone, and will continue to go, beyond their control; when they feel they are on the edge of a void, or up against a blank wall of fog.

But more than anything, they indicate a refusal to face the necessity for choice. What is their greatest need? It is to find a workable modern constitution for a nation with a very old political structure. The French, not daring to break with old habits to which they are deeply attached, are now being swept into the giddy current of modern technological advance. They are vaguely conscious that fundamental changes are on the way; that it is no longer a question of putting different men in power, or merely of replacing one form of Constitution by another, almost identical. They are entering a new phase of history, and once these things are set in motion there will be no going back. It is, to say the least, an impressive thought that France may be the first of the great powers called upon to show the world some kind of, still undefined, New Deal.

Anyone who produces new ideas will consequently be accused either of harking back to something too close to outworn and clearly outmoded formulae, or else of jettisoning tried and familiar methods in favour of reckless innovations.

There is more to it than this. As a nation, the French are quite willing to discuss and rethink when they feel that they are in control of the means and the pace of change. Now they feel

22

they have their backs to the wall. The door to the future may be blown open by a sudden squall at any moment. As a result as soon as anyone broaches the subject of a successor to the present régime, or begins to plan the changes this will entail, their minds turn inevitably to wondering what is going to happen and prophesying the events that might bring the Fifth Republic to an end. They want to take their decisions, or simply express their preferences in terms of these events. The argument is unrealistic and the outcome is, in fact, anyone's guess: de Gaulle will be assassinated—then the army will take over— or: the leaders of the Fourth Republic will come back to power —then the OAS will attempt a *putsch* . . . and so on.

These are sterile arguments, yet every living room, club and newspaper office is full of them and each one of us is only too ready to be drawn in. Far from clarifying the decisions that must be made, they tend to induce paralysis because they are based on purely hypothetical assumptions. We have no way of knowing in advance exactly how the change will come about, or when, or how long it will last, or what the conflicts and the cost will be.

This is why we must make a sharp distinction between the uncertainty about the upheavals which might attend the end of the Fifth Republic and the uncertainties about the exact nature of the system which follows. Contemplation of the first should on no account distract us from consideration of the second. We must think constructively about the future.

All groups, organisations and political parties are free to make their own guesses and draw their own conclusions about the moment of change, according to their separate goals. It is their job to rally their forces, keep them informed and lead them in such a way as to have a direct bearing on events. But it is always extremely difficult to forecast the future when power is in the hands of a single man. Should his prestige fall, or should he be unable to carry out his obligations to the full or, either by accident or from natural causes, be removed from the scene altogether—then the keystone is gone and the whole edifice collapses. No régime of this kind has ever been able to guarantee its succession by legal means: when the time has come they have always fallen to pieces. The people sense this and are instinctively wary of the moment when change will bring a break in continuity, clashes of opinion and maybe violent conflict. They are like invalids, unable to picture before the event the moment when they will walk again, hardly even daring to hope for it; but once on the road to recovery they trust in their new-found strength and are no longer scared of putting a foot to the ground.

At all events, however useful it may be to review the possibilities and estimate the relative forces involved, as a precaution against being caught at a disadvantage, this can never be more than guesswork, leading in turn to more guesswork and interminable argument. Such is not my intention here, for there are better things to do.

What *is* essential is that the great mass of the population—who may be called upon to act sooner than they expect—should know now that, whatever happens, and however the crisis comes about, there will have to be some form of interim government to keep in check any fascist pressures which may emerge, cope with any other difficulties that arise and set the stage for the new order. *Such a scheme will be unavoidable.* The situation calls for it and only the manner will depend on the conditions imposed by clearly unpredictable circumstances.

The Experiment still to be tried

What form will the new institutions take?

The argument has begun, but so far it has been subject to a certain amount of, perhaps not altogether unintentional, confusion. It is continually being thrown out of perspective by those people who say that, if you reject the present régime, or something very like it, this means returning to the Fourth Republic. This is not true. There is not necessarily a straight choice between personal power prolonged indefinitely and a return to an unworkable parliamentary system. We are not

24

forced to submit to this kind of blackmail. There are other ways out.

We can learn from our own past, as well as from the experience of other countries. It is not true that the French people are more difficult to govern than anyone else—always providing that they are not kept in the dark, that they are given a say in the measures being adopted and that their will is not consistently ignored and flouted by those governing them.

But is it possible to imagine real democracy flourishing within the existing economic framework? Isn't the entire project vitiated at the outset by the monopoly of certain controlling interests? Can we have a normal political life, a political life, that is, which is not bedevilled by the rackets to which we have grown accustomed, without completely transforming our economic structure, or at the very least substantially altering it?

The threat of pressure groups undoubtedly exists, and it is a very real threat. But no one will dispute that liberal institutions also give the forces of progress a chance to put their views across and give them a greater chance of succeeding than an authoritarian system. Indeed it is for this reason that certain factions resort to fascism and the *coup d'état* when they are afraid of losing ground. They know that a truly democratic society (and not one which merely pays lip service to democracy) provides a valid basis on which to build the reforms that progress and social justice demand.

More than that: such a democracy can only exist in the present century if it is backed by economic developments. It can only live and bear fruit if the nation is in a position to make its laws and authority respected in every field, especially the economic, which was formerly barred to it. The proposals set down here go beyond politics, therefore, into the realm of national economy.

Moreover these proposals pave the way for further, more sweeping developments. Once the state is more efficient, and therefore better able to command respect from numerous interests which today elude its authority, then reforms which

25

previous régimes were unable to accomplish become possible.

The up-to-date socialism of which so many Frenchmen dream, though they are not yet in a position to define it clearly, can be made reality by political democracy and a planned economy.

The Citizen's place in the Republic

There is more to democracy than simply placing a vote in the ballot box from time to time, delegating power to one of a number of elected representatives, and then sitting back in silence for the next five years and taking no further notice. The citizen must continue to take an active part in the affairs of the country as a whole, as well as those of his own locality and trade or profession. The rulers (whatever their platform), organisations, elected representatives and civil servants are exposed to pressure from every direction, and unless the watchful presence of the citizen makes itself felt, they are being abandoned to their own weaknesses. If that happens, then sooner or later they will give way either to the temptation of despotism or to a routine of so-called established rights. The only fluid and progressive society is one permeated by democratic ideals which are continually injecting fresh youth into the life of the community. Democracy is only efficient when it is total and permanent.

Salvation, then, will not come from above, either from one man or group of men or from any political parties, even if, as is to be hoped, many of them bring their own contributions to the fight. But when the people raise their voice there will be no gainsaying them. Once the people themselves choose the principles they want to govern their lives, they will override the troublesome minorities which are only dangerous when the masses are depressed, inarticulate and apathetic.

Of course, this awakening might well come too late, amid the dreadful chaos of civil war, letting loose a stream of violence in which both sides would inevitably provoke one another to further and further excesses. With the conflict would go the wholesale ruin of the country.

A race has begun, and from now on every person must wake up to his responsibilities. Men and women determined to prevent their country from being split by violence must band together, regardless of party and with no useless recriminations over the past, with the sole aim of smoothing over this transition to a new era.

I do not mean to advocate the kind of coalition which is made up of men fundamentally divided on every issue, who only unite in order to create a stalemate from which, in the end, it is always the people who suffer. I am calling for positive steps towards determining the new institutions of the country, and so opening the way for democratic socialism.

I firmly believe that this is possible—and I believe it more strongly than ever now that I have discussed it with four thousand interested Frenchmen.

It is for them that I have written this book. Not only because it is an attempt to answer the questions they asked me, but more than anything else, because this answer has grown out of their preoccupations and ideas.

CHAPTER TWO

THE FAILURE OF
THE LAST TWO REPUBLICS

A CLASSICAL argument for Frenchmen is: can political failures
be attributed solely to the wrong kind of government or are
they due to human nature?

Throughout his campaign against the old system de Gaulle
made it clear that he held the first view*. Léon Blum, on the
other hand, blamed politics and human weakness more than
the written provisions of the Constitution, and I am inclined to
share this opinion. It may also be conceded that both explanations are valid and complementary.

However if the country has settled for, and put up with an
unsuitable form of government for so long, if its chosen
representatives have failed in their task, and if their faults
have grown worse rather than better, there must be some
deeper reason for it. This is the first problem which this
chapter tries to solve.

Even granting that political formulae are only as useful as
politicians make them, it is worth considering whether one
kind of constitutional provision is more likely than another
to encourage or discourage deplorable habits and trends,
according to circumstances.

---

* That he did not, in fact, blame the men at the head of the
Fourth Republic is clear from his taking every opportunity to pay
tribute to them and gladly employing them in his own government.
This would indicate that their past failures were chiefly the result of
handicaps left over from the previous régime itself.

Two Unreal Democracies

Everyone condemns the Fourth French Republic for failing to carry out the increasingly heavy tasks which fall to the state. But there is also another case against it: the Fourth Republic claimed to be democratic and was not. The country was well aware that it was powerless to translate its will into fact, and each time the electorate was supposedly consulted the people felt that they had been cheated.

There is a connection between these two accusations. The people's will was constantly thwarted because their governments were weak, but also because, by failing to rely on the support of the country, timid governments deprived themselves of the only force which is capable today of overriding opposition. In so doing they prevented themselves from carrying out their tasks.

This was not how things looked to public opinion in general. When the very people who have been elected in order to carry out a given policy abandon it, they appear to be either cheats or weaklings. Moral condemnation is added to political disapproval and an impression tends to develop—carefully fostered by the enemies of the Republic—that, owing to some incurable, hidden flaw, this particular system allows only unworthy representatives to rise to power. This strikes at the very idea of democracy. Far from seeing that they have been let down by a betrayal of democratic ideals, too many people tend to hold democracy itself responsible. Confusion on this score has undoubtedly done more to humiliate the French people than a withdrawal from the colonial system which, following England's example and the lesson they themselves learned in Indo-China, they were prepared to consider ten years ago.

It is no wonder, then, that the leaders of the Fourth Republic found themselves alone and unarmed in the face of such attacks. Their own mistakes had deprived them of popular trust and support. A single push was enough to send them

29

packing when the time came, and no one raised a finger in their defence.

Thus the Fifth Republic was born. It is, undeniably, even less democratic than the Fourth. The French have no natural inclination to place unlimited power in the hands of a single individual. Having done so, for a short time and in what were considered exceptional circumstances, there is still a growing number who look with a certain amount of misgiving upon the road they have travelled. They are realising that every delicate situation, every incident, and every obstacle is being systematically exploited day after day by the President in order to strengthen the concept of personal power as the ultimate argument, the ultimate remedy for all the difficulties of the way.

Clemenceau waged a war and won it in respecting established institutions. Even though some of his decisions may not have been the right ones, he was able to govern without violating the Constitution, without article 16*, and with the cooperation of Parliament. Authority, in fact, is not derived from exceptional laws or arbitrary measures, but stems from actions carried out in the name of the people and with their full support. Churchill, in similar conditions, was able to make the most of his country's resources and lead it to victory against the most appalling odds.

In France during the past five years power has, on the contrary, become increasingly monopolised. The country—as it now realises very clearly—has never been associated with major decisions, despite occasional shows of consulting it by means of referendums which suggest a kind of Hobson's choice. The Evian agreement was certainly hailed with relief, but hardly with enthusiasm since the way to it was dark and strewn with ambiguous and contradictory statements. At no time was the nation's assistance sought or accepted.

The foundations of a régime contract in proportion to the increase in individual power. A faithful analysis of the

---

* For extracts from the text of the 1958 Constitution see Appendix on page 193.

referendum figures proves this, if, besides the *ouis* and *nons* written on the ballot papers, we take into account the reservations expressly formulated by a growing number of those who vote *oui*.

No less serious is the social unrest indicated by strikes and peasant movements; a sure sign that, despite increased productivity, our economic policy has aggravated the already unequal division of profits. *This is always the case in a country where public opinion has no legal means of making itself felt.*

Lastly, if de Gaulle has not been able to rule except by cheapening a Constitution which was, moreover, designed specifically for him, by abusing the powers it gave him and reducing the nation's representatives to the level of mere ciphers; if even this is not enough and the Constitution is still likely to be revised at a moment's notice, so that it can be amended tomorrow and replaced by another the day after, before it has even been put into practice. If this is so, then no one is going to take it seriously. No one is going to care how the letter of the law is used, violated or altered.

General de Gaulle himself may have a clear public image, and wide powers have been delegated to him personally, but the Fifth Republic and its institutions certainly have not. Does anyone take any notice of what deputies, ministers or high officials may say or do? Nowadays, when people are discussing politics, no one says: 'If I were the government . . .' They say: 'If I were de Gaulle . . .' Nothing reveals more clearly the uselessness of the 1958 Constitution.

Politics and Society

Strange as it may seem, the reasons for the failure of the Fourth and Fifth Republics have much in common.

In the first place there are sociological reasons. No régime can survive for long—much less succeed—unless it rests on a firm class structure, or on certain well defined layers of the population, unless it enjoys the active support of members able and willing to join in a common effort.

The Third Republic was upheld by the entire middle and lower middle class, in town and country. It satisfied their wishes. In France, throughout the first half of the twentieth century these classes suffered cruelly. They suffered proportionately more casualties than any other during the first World War. Then they were crushed by the burden of financial and economic chaos and lasting inflation—which were to have even more endurable effects. Between the two world wars they felt a constant threat to their privileges, security and even their very existence. Consequently they began to dissociate themselves from a political system which no longer afforded them protection. Not merely did they cease to serve and carry it, in the end they actually turned against it and, knowingly or unknowingly, behaved in a manner directly opposed to the interests of the community as a whole by reducing capital investment and adopting a foreign policy based on class ('rather Hitler than Léon Blum' for instance). The political and economic weakness of the last years of the Third Republic was the immediate result.

The Vichy period accentuated this imbalance by compromising most of the old guard and governing class with collaboration. At the Liberation, they were overwhelmed. But a fresh start was more difficult because no new stratum of society was ready to replace them, including from the working classes who were not prepared for the responsibility of running the country.

The Fourth Republic suffered from this state of affairs. The Fifth has not improved it. It has certainly tried to make use of technical experts from business, industry and the higher civil service, but they were quite unable to take the place of social groups spread throughout the nation as a whole, sustained by its vital strength, and alone capable of breathing life into a system to fit our times.

The structure of our society has been eaten away by economic and financial chaos and by persistent inflation—even though inflation has been punctuated by a few periods of deflation*. This situation paralysed progress and impeded the workings of a society which could only be based on an active and influential ruling class with a strong respect for its structural economic laws and a determination to make the state serve them. Most of those laws are the same for any highly developed industrial society, capitalist, semi-capitalist, socialist or totalitarian. For example, a healthy balance of supply and demand, or the channelling of savings, either spontaneous or induced, in favour of investments in the national interest, as it is seen in a particular place at a particular time. They must be accepted by the governing class both in its own behaviour and in the attitude it imposes on the state it governs. If they are not insuperable contradictions are bound to arise.

Of course, it does happen that a chance swing or accident of events can temporarily disguise a dangerous instability. Then to all appearances there is a period of peaceful optimism. But the difficulties and crises have not really vanished. This is true of any country, whatever its legal and social organisation. The Russians are well aware of this, and they make constant efforts to direct their financial affairs with a strictness that many a capitalist country might envy.

When the normal interplay of various economic factors has been disrupted by particular historical circumstances, the damage cannot be repaired in a day. France has not yet finished with the effects of half a century of economic disorders, crises and destruction of wealth, with all their psychological, moral and political consequences. The structures and forces capable of establishing a prosperous modern state must be rebuilt stone by stone. It is our job to decide what there structures should be and to speed up their installation.

The men at the head of the Fourth and Fifth Republics have lacked the imagination to do this. They failed to understand the necessities of their time and therefore did nothing to meet

---

* Whose cost has, moreover, been borne by the same sections of society and more especially, by the working class in general.

33

them. In this they revealed a conservative mentality: they were unaware of the problem, and instead of taking the long term view which would have demanded sweeping changes, each in his own way was satisfied, more often than not, to maintain old habits and beliefs and ways of government incompatible with economic and social progress. This is at the root of young people's dissatisfaction with both régimes and their leaders.

In point of fact, neither one nor the other was in a position to cope with these problems, or even to begin to deal with them in a satisfactory way.

The organisation of the Fourth Republic, like that of the Fifth, was based, indeed, on patterns inherited from the previous century, a period when, except on rare occasions, members of the administration limited their activities strictly to political matters; when, consequently, the only basis of democracy was the presentation of a number of conflicting ideologies. In the twentieth century this is no longer the case. Ministers and all public bodies are continually called upon to settle disputes between different economic interests, to make decisions aimed at stimulating production or export trade, to modernise industry and agriculture, regulate wages and credit, and so forth. Neither the Fourth nor Fifth Republics have been equipped to assume these new responsibilities. In other circumstances such a hiatus could have been bearable, but this has been an era of reconstruction, of the beginnings of economic planning, of freer exchange and trade and the Common Market. None of these tests could be met and overcome successfully by means of day-to-day improvisation or incoherent wishful thinking. They could be dealt with only by a conscious and co-ordinated effort.

In any event, the mere existence of an Economic Council, acting in a purely advisory capacity, is certainly not enough. Neither governments nor Parliaments have ever recognised that it had any real authority, or granted its opinions their due weight. Economic debates in Parliament have been consistently dominated, or at least influenced to a large extent, by electoral considerations. Finally, the economic standing of politicians and the general level of information throughout the country has remained mediocre.

These facts go a long way to explain inadequate increases in productivity, as well as improvements in our standards of living. For we must not be misled by the euphoric pronouncements with which we are lulled. Our progress has not kept pace with the nation's efforts, or with those of its workers. Germany, Italy and the Netherlands (our neighbours and direct competitors in the Common Market) have risen more swiftly. It is vital that in future the maximum use should be made of the work of all productive sections of the community, and that the rewards should be more fairly and realistically distributed. This is a fundamental objective and one which should be taken into consideration when it comes to incorporating the nation's vital forces into the workings of a truly democratic state*.

The Absence of a Counterweight

The parallel between the two régimes can also be carried over on to a political plane. In any system of government an efficient division of labour and responsibility can be achieved by organised relations between the various authorities, each with its own particular sphere of influence. Both the Fourth and Fifth Republics were characterised equally by a total lack of equilibrium between the principal state organisations: the Assemblies and the executive powers.

Under the Fourth Republic all power was effectively concentrated in the hands of the National Assembly. Besides exercising the power of legislation the Assembly was able to paralyse government action by various legal and other devices. The executive existed under the constant threat of having its decisions countermanded; it was deprived of any prospect of continuity and was thus incapable of displaying a will of its own.

---

* See Chapter Five, p 73.

It was trying to reconcile incompatible interests and at the same time giving way to the pressures that harried it. The price of these attempts was total immobility. For all practical purposes no government worthy of the name existed. A dozen men calling themselves ministers sat in the seats of power, but they did not constitute a government. They enjoyed no margin of freedom or time in their everyday work and in the end they could make no decisions, start no new undertakings and finish none of the tasks they were supposed to do.

Public opinion was shocked by the frequent ministerial crises, but, even between crises, the debilitated state of the government prevented it from taking any real action*.

The Fifth Republic contains the same flaw, but in reverse. This time it is the head of state who, not content with hampering the executive, is arrogating a part of the legislation to himself by manipulating, or actually infringing the Constitution, and reducing Parliament to a subsidiary rôle.

The 1958 Constitution completely reversed the republican tradition in which Parliament is the statutory legislative body, the government intervening only as a secondary measure—either when Parliament has taken no decision or acting on authority delegated by it. The realm of parliamentary legislation is now defined by means of limiting clauses: article 34 of the Constitution contains a list of matters on which the assemblies are considered fit to lay down 'rules' or 'basic

---

* 'In thirteen years,' writes Etienne Hirsch, former High Commissioner for Planning, 'I was associated with twenty-three governments, in various capacities: as a member of the Planning Commission, and later as its Chairman. This meant that there were different governments in power for the Plan's initiation, its discussion in Parliament and finally for the period when it was put into operation. A great deal of time was taken up in explaining to ministers living under the threat of a dissolution or a crisis of some kind, what were the proper plans to make for the next four years, and time and again I had the impression that the minister I was talking to was busy wondering if I had the slightest idea of his real position.'

principles'*. By virtue of article 37 all other matters come within the jurisdiction of the government alone. Thus the government exercises wide statutory powers in complete independence of Parliament, even to the extent of modifying or amending laws which were formerly subject to act of Parliament.

Consequently, as Professor Rivero has observed, it is the government which becomes the normal and common legislator, the principal legislative body; while Parliament is able to legislate only in so far as the power is explicitly delegated to it. It is thus reduced to the rôle of 'legislator by assign', only in special and limited circumstances.

Furthermore, when Parliament cannot legislate officially on matters which henceforth come within the government's jurisdiction, then government legislation may well encroach on parliamentary matters: all that is needed is an enabling clause, such as that provided for in article 38 of the Constitution, which can suspend parliamentary powers of legislation for an indefinite period. Moreover, these rules are applied in a particularly extensive spirit. Many students have commented on the timid interpretation given to the text of the Constitution as a whole by the president of the National Assembly. One of them, Léon Hamon, draws attention to his 'caution' and points out that he always preferred 'to keep well within the limits of his legislative powers (rather) than risk another clash with the Constitutional Council'. There has never been any doubt of this Council's conciliatory attitude towards the executive and on more than one occasion it has ruled that one of the assemblies has overstepped its authority in legislating on some subject which it declared to be within the government's province.

The executive is also within its rights in ratifying a budget if this has not been finally passed by both chambers within

---

* These are, admittedly, both numerous and important, but that is beside the point. For a translation of the text of these articles see Appendix pp. 193-205.

seventy days of its presentation—clearly a considerable increase in the government's legislative powers*.

Is there, in fact, any longer any real point in talking about 'the government' and its prerogatives? A government, properly speaking, with a personality of its own, no longer exists, thanks to the application of principles already built into the Constitution, or to the repeated extension of them in daily practice. During the Fourth Republic the government may have been to all intents and purposes absorbed in the Assembly: today it is absorbed in the person of the head of state. Policy is conceived, adopted and carried out by one man only. If he lacks the time or inclination to deal with a particular problem he will delegate it to a minister or to one of his close advisors: their job is to interpret the president's wishes in much the same way as their predecessors tried to follow the views of certain political parties or lobbies.

But Parliament cannot lightly be dispensed with. An active Parliament serves as a check on the government, forcing it to explain its policies to the public, to publish the facts for discussion and give an account of its progress. In other words parliamentary questions are the basis of a free flow of information. The history of France, like that of other countries, teaches us that every kind of freedom is equally bound up with the existence of a respected Parliament.

'Unlimited power is madness. . . . A people is free to the precise extent that it exercises its own sovereignty and declines to leave it in the hands of one Assembly, one Party or one man. . . .' This dictum of the philosopher Alain, quoted by Professor Vedel, applies equally to the Fourth and Fifth Republics. Both of them have overlooked the necessity for a

* Another well known fact is that article 16 of the Constitution authorises the President of the Republic to take any steps he considers necessary, if the circumstances appear to him to justify them. Article 11 also empowers him to amend civil and common law by use of referenda. He has even 'interpreted' this clause as a justification for proposing to revise the Constitution by means of a referendum, without previously consulting Parliament.

balanced division of duties and prerogatives and, as a result, we can see that both of them have progressed with increasing speed towards a monopoly of power: yesterday by the National Assembly, today by the head of state. Yesterday we were moving towards anarchy; today we are heading for despotism. What is lacking in both cases has been balanced co-operation, a counterweight, which other nations have been able to supply. In both cases power has been almost entirely one-sided, and as a result the entire administration is unbalanced. In both cases, however dissimilar they may appear, the effect has been the same: a weak, wavering system which the country does not understand, and which it puts up with but does not believe in.

Public opinion was admittedly able to make itself felt during the Fourth Republic by the way people voted. From time to time it has also been satisfied under the Fifth (the peace in Algeria is one example of this). But it has never been able to control events and obtain satisfaction at the same time. It has never been able to initiate and watch over its own chosen policy from the beginning, to see its own views expressed in action and feel pride in its sovereignty, first in the decision taken and then in the way it is carried out. Under the Fourth Republic the people felt cheated; under the Fifth they feel they are being treated like children. What is certain is that they may allow themselves to be treated like children today, out of disgust at the frauds practised on them yesterday, but they will not allow it for ever.

If we hope to provide the France of tomorrow with a system of government which on the one hand guarantees the electorate's effective participation in determining policy, and on the other ensures efficiency and continuity in carrying it out, it is essential that a correct balance of power should be achieved. Montesquieu, two centuries ago, put the matter in a nutshell. *'Give any man'* (and I would add, any organised body of men) *'power and he is naturally tempted to abuse it; he will carry it as far as he can. . . . If the abuse of power is to be prevented, things must be arranged so that power checks power.'*

39

Democracy lies in the correct balance of power. In itself such a balance is democracy.

The Rôle of Parliament and Its Limitations

When the time comes to correct the Fifth Republic's errors, we shall have to take care not to fall back into the mistakes of the Fourth. The idea of putting up bars to prevent the abuse of executive power has a natural appeal to the left. This is because the fight for liberty and emancipation was originally fought against the king and his ministers. It was necessary to resist them, limit their prerogatives, make them submit to the authority of a Parliament whose rights needed constant reinforcement. Throughout the last century the people's elected assemblies were confronted by governments composed of eminent conservatives whose mission and inclinations were to hold back popular pressure. Moving in the direction of this pressure meant at first a struggle against established power. This power had to be weakened before the people could be heard.

The tradition which grew up then is still alive today in France. It is at the root of the reluctance shown by many socialists and republicans to commit themselves to ensuring a stable government.

But it would be a mistake to imagine that democracy can be extended by methods which paralyse the workings of the State at a time when those who speak for it ought to have the necessary means at their disposal to hold their own against private interests and economic and financial pressure.

It is perfectly true—as de Gaulle (echoing Montesquieu) has recently confirmed—that, because it possesses physical power and is in command of the administration, the police, the army, television and radio links etc. and because it holds the purse strings, the executive may yield to the temptation to act in an undemocratic way. It is a truism that 'power corrupts' and all too often ends in despotism. But we must not set the executive as it is, or might become, against the legislature as it should be.

After all, the Assemblies also have their weaknesses and we know only too well that they are apt to slide into demagogy, intrigue and infringements of government action. There are pressure groups and lobbies to be found in the corridors of the assemblies just as much as in ministerial waiting rooms.

The balance of power has shifted from the Assembly to the executive. We must not, in France, simply shift it back to where it was.

Parliament is important because it stands for the will of the people: it is, first and foremost, a representative body. It represents the differing ideals and political theories which form public opinion when facing questions of policy. In dealing with clashing interests and the problems raised by economic policy, it represents social and professional forces*.

It is precisely because Parliament represents the will of the nation that it should supervise the government's execution of the country's chosen policy. For the same reason it frames laws to fit it: in principle the representative and legislative powers are one and the same. They should be separate from the executive. The division of power is one way of achieving the constitutional balance we have shown to be necessary.

All the same, this division cannot be absolute. The will expressed by the assemblies only exists to the full in its application. Its decisions must be put into practice; but this cannot be done by five or six hundred deputies. To carry out the decisions a limited number of men working together as a team are needed. This is a basic condition for getting anything done.

The two principal organs of state are therefore formed for co-operation. Liaison between them is unavoidable; they are constantly acting and reacting against one another. Certain realms of activity belong, properly speaking, to one or the other, but in fact they are inevitably shared. It is the same with the actual task of legislation which, in our time, has become

---

* For further discussion of the representation of social and professional forces, see Chapter Five, p. 73.

extremely weighty, complex and fluid and sometimes demands the utmost speed. Consequently in France, as in other countries, the assemblies have tended to allow the government to act in matters which formerly belonged to them alone. This is often the case in the economic field which today is becoming one of the State's most important spheres of action. The policy agreed on between Parliament and the government can only be carried out if the latter is given wide latitude, guaranteeing it the necessary time and elbow room.

The will of the people has been thwarted time and again in the past because the government lacked the means to make it law. This was the case with Herriot's government (in 1925) and Léon Blum's (in 1937 and 1938), both of which were forced to resign in the face of political and financial coalitions, even though it was well known that the country was with them. If they had had the right to dissolve Parliament they would not have fallen. The same observation applies to another government, twenty years later, which lasted only seven months and seventeen days*. If these governments had still been overthrown, they would have gone to the country and the electorate would have returned them to power with increased majorities. The people would have had the last word. Thus, far from weakening democracy, the reinforcement of governmental powers can allow it to express itself more effectively.

We can often answer criticism of the parliamentary system as practised during the Fourth Republic by saying that it died of too little democracy rather than too much. In fact, there was too little democracy because the policy the country wanted was not carried out. But this was not due to limitations in the power of the assemblies. The fact was that it was often the executive which had insufficient power.

---

* The author was prime minister of France from 19 June 1954 to 5 February 1955. *Translator's note.*

The part played by the Individual Citizen

But when it comes to overcoming major difficulties or resolving conflicting doctrines or interests, is it possible to rely entirely on legal or institutional provisions, however well conceived, or on deputies and ministers, however well intentioned? Can a democratic state survive unless the majority of individual citizens take an active part in the conduct of affairs?

The answer to these questions is no, because democracy is not localised at the top, and the ballot paper remains nothing more than a symbol if the citizen is satisfied with such a situation. The will of the nation can prevail only if the people exercise their rights directly in the countless local and national organisations which deal with all matters affecting the life of the community. 'The degree of democracy in a given country can be measured by its inhabitants' degree of participation in all matters of public interest, that is to say, in affairs which affect the life of the community and are not strictly personal or family matters.' (Pierre Belleville.)

Over the past twenty years there has been a consistent lack of this kind of democratic irrigation in all aspects of public life, in France, and this is both the cause and effect of the deficiencies described above. But it is also a lesson for the future. It is not enough to re-establish the appearance of democracy: in order to build a real democracy we need the help of every single individual. Unless people constantly play their parts as citizens to the full, there will be no democracy.

CHAPTER THREE

THE CONCEPT OF
PERSONAL POWER

EVERYONE IS aware of the need for a strong, permanent executive. The reason de Gaulle has met with so little opposition in his rise to power is that the people had finally become so exasperated by weak and unstable governments that they were prepared to try out any solution so long as it put an end to the previous chaos.

Stability, even more than efficiency, was the keynote of the promoters of the Fifth Republic*. (Efficiency, though more important, is a more difficult achievement to prove.) Every speech made by de Gaulle on any subject always culminated with the ominous threat of an inescapable return to the weakness of the Fourth Republic—the ghost of all those evils which still haunt the country. This was what was in store for the nation if they answered *non* to him.

Each time the question arises of granting still wider powers

---

* A stability, despite all appearances, which is purely relative. Beside the Debré-Pompidou change of government there have been countless ministerial reshuffles since 13 May 1958. In five years we have had seven Ministers of Education, three Finance Ministers, seven Ministers of Information, three Keepers of the Seals, and so on. Yet so long as de Gaulle seems to be the one person really in charge, most people do not worry about these changes and permutations, regarding them as of secondary importance, although they offer just as much of a threat to the government's efficiency and continuity as did similar changes under the Fourth Republic.

to the head of state, the need for stability is again invoked as a justification.

In this way the present system is carried away by its own logic and tends to overstretch itself more every day. The 1958 Constitution gives the President of the Republic both extremely wide legislative powers and the right to dissolve Parliament. The twists given to this constitution by the wide interpretation of article 16 and by a whole series of other abuses plus a servile Constitutional Council which unfailingly favours the executive and which, in the celebrated phrase, gives favours instead of judgments* have been succeeded by new and ever more far-reaching projects.

This tendency was denounced as early as 1933 by René Capitant in his study of systems of parliamentary government. He emphasised the need to 'separate the idea of a strong government from that of a powerful head of state. In French political theory the two ideas are all too often confused. As a result of this confusion, any movement towards reinforcing the executive power is inevitably directed towards strengthening the prerogatives of the president. Such a tendency works against the interests of parliamentary government. Orléanist politics were already out of date in 1875 and they cannot be revived in France.'

Public opinion is beginning to realise that by gradually allowing all power to accumulate in the hands of one man the country is moving irresistibly towards despotism—and that despotism, however benevolent in fact, always ends by falling into the situation described by de Gaulle himself in his celebrated speech at Bayeux in June 1956:

---

* By some miracle of sleight of hand, the Constitutional Council has been presented as a replica of the United States Supreme Court. But the Supreme Court in America protects the rights of the individual against the state, while in France the citizen has no means of access to the Council at all. In fact it is the President who makes use of the Council to ratify his own encroachments and the constant extension of his powers, as well as to place more and more restrictions on what is left of parliament.

'To begin with it (dictatorship) certainly looks promising. Thanks to a glittering backdrop of one-way propaganda and a background of enthusiasm from some and resignation from others, it imposes strict discipline and initially produces an impression of dynamic energy which contrasts favourably with the anarchy that went before. But dictatorship is fated to over-estimate its achievements. . . . Obstacles rise from outside and from within, and multiply at every step. Finally the spring breaks. The imposing edifice collapses in blood and wretchedness. The nation emerges broken, sunk lower even than before the experiment began.'

History bears out this lesson. Experiments in personal power have always followed the same pattern of development and decay.

The Presidential Régime

A number of politicians and lawyers are endeavouring to pro-mote a more balanced régime which, while consolidating the executive, would nevertheless safeguard the rights of Parlia-ment. Many of them support the presidential régime and quote America as a precedent.

In the United States the head of state is also the head of the government; the existence and integrity of the two powers, the executive and the legislative, are guaranteed by the fact that they are completely independent of one another and are of equal importance. Both are elected by universal suffrage, but the President cannot dissolve Congress, nor can Congress over-throw the President. The head of state is elected by the nation and directly responsible to it. But only the House of Repre-sentatives and the Senate can pass laws, authorise expenditure, ratify treaties and so forth, and there is no way of bypassing their consent.

The partisans of a presidential régime are in agreement with that of de Gaulle in the election of the President by universal suffrage—a method of election which they regard as permissible once Parliament is no longer ruled by the head of state. On the other hand they would restore all legislative power to Parliament, make it necessary for it to approve the budget, abolish broad provisions like those of article 16 and article 37, and protect the National Assembly from the threat of dissolution. In other words, their system attempts to introduce an overall balance, symmetry and stability which are totally lacking from the régime chosen by General de Gaulle.

It is worth trying to imagine how a presidential system would function in a country such as France.

How, under this system, would conflicts between the two elected chambers and the President, and disputes between the chambers themselves, be resolved? When confronted by an Assembly whose very nature prevents it from being monolithic, since it represents the divided opinions of the country, is there not a great temptation for one man, who has been swept into power by the electorate, to use the very real power and considerable political prestige at his disposal against other institutions, and so against the interests of freedom?

Unless the Constitution provides some means of settling such disagreements, unless one of the authorities has the right to impose its will on the others and so prevent a situation arising to which there is no legal solution, there must be a risk of encouraging irresistibly a man who is sure of his popularity and has at his disposal all the modern means of communication to abuse his trump cards in order to overcome opposition. Should he himself hesitate to do this, it is easy to imagine the pressure that would be brought to bear on him by his Party and his advisors who would be continually obsessed by the fear of losing the next election. A statesman, after all, is always sincerely convinced that his policy is the best one. Under these conditions how could he possibly resist the desire to pursue this policy at all costs, even if it meant a few incursions into illegality?

The United States is the only country in the world in which

the presidential system has ever worked normally. But, apart from the danger of acting on the inspiration of a single precedent, it must be clearly understood that the United States is a federal state and therefore there is no risk of the President's acquiring too much personal power. For many years the President of the United States possessed only very limited powers: the real authority, financial control and the machinery of administration were in the hands of the different states. This was the framework within which the system was first drafted and began to work. There has certainly been a gradual increase in presidential powers; but the initial context is always very important to the life of any political system, and here it differs profoundly from that of France. Then again, presidential powers in the United States are still limited today. If the President of the United States should wish to overstep his rights he would find the elected governors and assemblies of the majority of the states aligned against him, with their administrative bodies, police forces, radio and television stations, financial resources and so on. There would be a new war of secession, in which the President would be defeated from the outset. For this reason disputes between the White House and the Capitol can only lead, at the worst, to stagnation and immobility and the deferment of decisions and reforms. There are countless examples of this in the history of the United States, and it is really remarkable that the advocates of a presidential régime have never taken any notice of them. But everything goes to show that the American system would take on quite a different and a singularly disturbing appearance if it were transplanted to a strongly centralised country such as France: instead of stagnation and immobility it would lead to an explosion. ∞

The last and most serious objection to this régime is that, beneath the democratic façade of a dual election, there is a very real risk of draining the lifeblood from the country's democratic spirit and activity.

When the people elect an Assembly they are voting for

parties whose principles they already know, at least as far as general policy is concerned; they are choosing specific programmes and proposals. When, on the other hand, the electorate places one man at the head of the state they are voting for him personally. Literally they 'put their trust in him', they rely on him, and they sometimes do so on the basis of more or less spurious promises. In this respect American presidential campaigns tend towards a mediocrity which one hardly wishes to see imported into France.

An election of this kind cannot provide an authentic element of political control; it even tends to make the electorate lose interest in politics, encourages it to abdicate, to develop the habit of not exercising its rights and of taking little interest in the affairs of state. At a time like the present, nothing could be more dangerous. Encourage the nation in the belief that everything will be decided without its intervention, and you present an unlooked-for chance for adventurers. You protect them from the only force able to hold them in check: a people which has made its choice between the policies and solutions put to it, and which means to see that its choice is respected.

The French Context

Certain other conditions of French political life cannot be passed over in silence when the presidential system is under consideration. De Gaulle has created a number of precedents: by reducing the position of the Assemblies; by the use he has made of the Constitution and by the interpretation he has given to it, and imposed on it by his use of the referendum. If a presidential system based on the American pattern were to be established in France tomorrow, it would be very difficult to persuade the next President to move backwards. It is true to say that, by his abuses and exaggerations, de Gaulle has made any attempt at an authentic, balanced presidential system even more difficult.

Moreover, in France today the election of a head of state by means of universal suffrage presents other difficulties which

49

stem from the present division of public opinion. The American system is based on the existence of two huge parties engaged in a struggle for power. Because of this the presidential election can, in fact, be summed up by a ballot. This gives the system an undoubted clarity and avoids many tiresome combinations and intrigues. In France, the bulk of the electorate is split up into numerous parties, and although everyone deplores this fact, it cannot be remedied; or at least not from one day to the next. This proliferation of parties makes it impossible to elect a president after a single ballot and all sorts of arrangements and concessions are inevitable between ballots. Even so, there is nothing to show that the president will obtain an absolute majority, or that a candidate whose initial poll was very small might not scrape in and consequently be unable to face strong oppositions throughout his term of office. This is something which has often been criticised in local elections; in this limited field, it presents only very minor inconveniences after all but it becomes very serious on a national level. This is no way to choose the supreme arbiter of the nation, the symbol of unity and of the will of the people.

If we study these hypotheses still more closely, it is not difficult to predict that candidates in a nation-wide contest will try to mobilise the greatest possible number of votes by resorting to the kind of over-simplified arguments which have already proved their worth in earlier campaigns. For the spokesman or spokesmen of the right, anti-communism is a convenient way of side-stepping more awkward subjects, as well as a way of uniting moderates and extremists and helping to win over doubtful or nervous voters from the centre. It is easy and tempting to denounce the red peril—not so much with a view to damaging a Communist candidate who stands no chance of being elected but to dissuade the electors from giving their vote to a socialist or democratic candidate who, it is implied, will receive the floating Communist vote in the second round and is therefore as good as in the pay of Moscow*.

Bearing in mind the political habits of this country and the place on the chess board occupied by the Communist Party—too limited to present an actual danger, but important enough to arouse fears (fears which are, moreover, constantly fed by right wing propaganda)—it is clear that the whole electoral campaign will depend on this issue. There will be no mention of planning, of European unity, or of economic reform. Good Frenchmen will be called upon, between two demagogic promises, to unite against the men from Moscow, those who openly admit to being so and those who hide it, those who are suspected of seeking or accepting support from the extreme left in the second stage of the ballot or of giving it theirs. This is the kind of constructive, high-level politics the country will be offered: such unedifying behaviour will never mould public opinion on sensible lines.

There is no possibility of avoiding this trap. The Communist Party represents some twenty to twenty-five per cent of the electorate, so that its candidate will come fairly high up in the poll and will always be in a good position to play a decisive part in the second round of an election. This is another fact which can neither be denied nor ignored.

Some distinguished theorists, Professor Vedel and Professor Duverger amongst them, maintain that the Communist vote in the first ballot will not reach twenty or twenty-five per cent of the electorate and that, as their electoral influence is smaller, the consequences I have described will become less likely. This theory—which, in any case, is mere supposition—is not at all convincing. Nothing will stop the right wing parties and press from basing their campaign on 'the Communist peril' and 'its allies'. Nor will anything stop the Communist voters

---

* The recent revision of the Constitution, which restricts the second ballot to the two candidates who topped the poll in the first, is useless. Whether we like it or not, the Communist Party will be compelled to direct its share of the electorate to vote for either candidate X or Y, with the inevitable result that polemics and smear campaigns will develop along the lines described above.

from doing their best to make their wishes felt—even though they know their candidate cannot finally be elected—by voting for him in the first round, placing the party of their choice as high as possible in the poll and so helping to make the best political bargain of their withdrawal from the second ballot. This is perfectly legitimate reasoning and conforms, moreover, to the tradition in which everyone makes the most of his chances in the first ballot, although well aware that only the second will be decisive.

What would be the final result? The easily aroused fear of Communism would, as is intended, lead to a mass movement from the centre and left of centre towards the right.

The left will soon realise this and half the country will reject a system which gives its views no chance. Also the right will have a permanent advantage and a hold on the executive, and if the National Assembly is left wing, conflict between it and the President will be inevitable from the very first day.

Those who advocate a presidential system are therefore endangering the whole political future of the nation in their anxiety to strengthen the executive without departing from the ways traced—whether they like it or not—by Gaullism, rather than by looking for a solution in some other direction. Without realising it, they are moving backwards to the Bonapartist orbit which has dogged the country persistently for the last century and a half and has led to catastrophic set-backs each time it has come to the fore.

Commitment or Abdication

I know that many people are bewildered by the echoes which come back to them from the past and are impatient, above all, to achieve efficiency and recovery. They are therefore turning towards formulae which, because they are supposed new in France, seem to offer guarantees against a return to weakness and impotence. We have a duty to put people on their guard against an illusion which tomorrow will prove to be yet another disappointment.

One fashionable idea which they have been told they must accept is the 'personalisation of political life'. Radio broadcasts, newsreels and television networks carry the voices and faces of political personalities like those of film stars into the most remote parts of the country. The listener or viewer feels as though he is in direct contact with these personalities; he knows them and lives with them. In the end constant repetition of picture and sound acts independently of the sense of what is being said and their subconscious effect is like that of an advertising slogan. A president is 'sold' like a brand of cigarettes or toothpaste. Gradually, along with the product, the need for the product is induced. It is a familiar modern phenomenon in the advertising world.

Yet, even in the commercial field, all of us must at some time have realised the excessive power of advertising. It is common knowledge that subliminal techniques are occasionally practised on the consumer. Everyone admits that such tendencies ought to be checked and the more responsible elements in the profession are the first to condemn them.

Is this the moment, in a field as serious as politics, to encourage methods which have already been severely criticised elsewhere and to adopt certain kinds of institution which are dangerously likely to stimulate them?

In one sense, admittedly, political life has always been a matter of personalities; it could hardly be otherwise since politics are not merely made by men, but consist of men's reactions to other men. Once a painter or writer has imparted his own style and turn of mind to his work he can, if need be, wipe out his own life and personality completely. The politician, on the other hand, acts out his own work all the time; the tools of his trade are his whole personality. The political work of Robespierre or Jaurès during their lifetimes was no more nor less than the men themselves.

Nevertheless, for those who came after them, Robespierre and Jaurès were principally a collection of ideas, they represented certain objectives and the use of certain methods to achieve them—they introduced and stood for a policy and their supporters chose them precisely because they agreed with it.

If we adopt a policy and trust one man rather than another to carry it out, because he is the one who is the most suitable and most worthy, this also involves reserving the right to judge him by his deeds. This is exactly what it means to behave like a responsible citizen. It has nothing to do with putting oneself entirely in the hands of a man and leaving him to solve every problem in his own way.

Jaurès said: 'It is the right of the common people, it is the right of the oppressed to read our lives and our consciences like an open book. And when the common people understand all the politicians thoroughly they will see that they must never abandon themselves completely to any one man. All of us, however well-meaning, can stumble and make mistakes at some time.'

I am not one of those who ignore the fruitful or catastrophic part which a single man can play in public affairs. No one has been more severely critical of those who have misgoverned the country and betrayed its interests. It is my deepest and most patriotic wish that the country, too, will judge them harshly and make better choices tomorrow. But all its decisions should be based, first and foremost, on a precise knowledge of what it wants, on determined objectives and clearly stated contracts.

If the people choose a leader purely on the grounds of his talent, deserts and prestige (or because of his electoral skill), they are abdicating and renouncing their right to govern themselves. This is a retrograde step in terms of the evolution which history has taught us to look upon as progress.

PART TWO

PROPOSALS

The Republic is a tool
JAURÈS

So FAR everything that has been discussed has been negative and aimed at clearing the ground. Now we must turn to constructive proposals.

The problem facing the French people today is to obtain a stable and, above all, an efficient government within the framework of a true, working democracy. How can this be achieved?

My investigations have confirmed that opinions are divided on this score. Nevertheless the objectives aimed at by the majority of Frenchmen are the same and it must be possible to find solutions which are acceptable if not to all, then at least to the greatest number.

Obviously no miracle formula exists; there is no legal system which incorporates all the advantages and none of the disadvantages. There is no perfect régime. Nor are there any institutions which cannot be used or manipulated improperly.

Institutions are embodied in the men whose job it is to make them work. Whatever precautions are taken to bring about balanced cooperation between the various authorities and reconcile opposing forces, it always comes back to men. Just because they are not perfect, and because there are groups with conflicting interests, everyone, from the man in the street to the head of state, always tends to use institutions for his personal advantage, or that of his own party or class.

None the less, we can and must endeavour to forearm our-selves against possible deviations, to place obstacles in the way of abuses, and reduce temptation and sharp practices. This is my particular target in Chapter Four which is concerned with political institutions as such and tries to establish the proper rôle and rights of Parliament, the function of the executive, the way in which the two bodies can be made to work together and how to arbitrate between them.

In Chapter Five I shall study the composition of the assemblies with the object of representing faithfully not only the country's political families but also the social groups and economic interests which are vital to the functioning of a modern nation and a planned economy.

Chapter Six examines other political aspects of a type of planning which would be democratic in its aims and methods. Chapter Seven goes on to deduce the consequences for pro-ductive enterprises, both private and public—and Chapter Eight, the rôle of the unions in a planned economy in general, and in relation to industry in particular.

The new organisation demands extensive decentralisation and a policy of regional and rural regeneration. This is dealt with in Chapter Nine.

The economic organisations to be set up on a national or regional scale should not be in any way subsidiary or purely technical institutions. They must be thoroughly alive and endowed with responsibilities and powers of decision. There-fore they must necessarily spring from democratic roots and be fully representative of the various social and professional interests, especially those of the classes which contribute most actively to productivity and to regenerating and stimulating the life of the community.

It must never be forgotten that democracy is not merely a fixture or an ingenious mechanical arrangement of institutions unconnected with individual citizens (whether the citizens have given them passive support or actively approved them). Democracy must permeate collective activity in all its aspects and at all levels. It needs the participation of the greatest possible number wherever and whenever possible. Chapter Ten is devoted to this fundamental principle: in it I have tried to determine what part the citizen should play in the life of the city.

All these proposals have been designed to meet the demands of the contract made between the nation and its representatives and to ensure that this contract shall be fully carried out.

CHAPTER FOUR

THE EXECUTIVE
AND PARLIAMENT

THERE IS no democracy if the executive governs uncontrolled
by the representative power, since the latter speaks in the name
of the country and must see that its wishes are respected.

But parliamentary control should not be all-embracing to
the point of inhibiting the actions of the executive. The
executive must be independent, lasting and possess the means
to carry out its duties without being paralysed.

It is difficult to reconcile the needs of an independent
executive and control by the representative power, but it is
not impossible. A dozen or more countries throughout the
world at a stage of development similar to France, have
achieved it.

The Balance of Power

If Parliament is to be able to exercise its function in the name
of the electorate for which it stands, it must have two acknow-
ledged attributes:

1 It must play a part in the appointment and constitution
of the government so that the government may be set up in
accordance with the will of the people; and it must be able to
question, challenge and censure the government.

Montesquieu, the accredited spokesman for divided authority, has no hesitation in claiming that 'the legislative power

. . . has the right, and should have the means, of examining the way in which its laws are being carried out'.

2 It must be responsible for transforming the nation's will into law. Article 34 of the present Constitution, which makes the government 'the legislator of common law'*, is unacceptable for precisely this reason.

Responsibility for legislation must be restored to Parliament, with one reservation. It must be able, if need arises, to delegate to the government the power to take such decisions as normally fall within the jurisdiction of Parliament, when this is necessary to the pursuit of a mutually agreed policy which figures in the 'majority agreement' (I shall discuss this point later). In this way Parliament could authorise the government to amend the law in specific fields and for a specific period of time.

On the other hand, members of Parliament must share the right of initiating legislation with the government, and every deputy must be able to bring in bills; the majority must recover their right to table motions, even against government opposition (with the traditional reservations limiting parliamentary initiative in cases of increased expenditure or reduction in income).

The right of challenge and censure on the one hand, and the right of initiating legislation on the other, implies that each Assembly must control its own agenda. The government must also be able to table motions about projects it considers important, but without going so far as to monopolise parliamentary time.

Given a Parliament whose scope and dignity has been guaranteed in this way, the government, for its part, ought to possess the means and the time necessary to carry out the terms of the 'majority agreement'. This was not the case under the Fourth Republic, or even the Third. In our time the weakness of the

---

* See Chapter Two, pages 36 to 39

state and those who have guided it, far from being a guarantee of democratic freedom, has led, in fact, to making them only more vulnerable to the pressure of minority interests.

The way to avoid having a precarious and unstable government without falling into dictatorship lies in a solution closely linking the government's functions, tasks and duration with the functions, tasks and duration of the Assembly.

When a general election brings in a new National Assembly, a government should be formed in accordance with the majority vote, and, in principle, this government should last as long as the Assembly itself. This formula, with slight variations, is practised in all the countries where parliamentary democracy works more or less satisfactorily, whatever the country's sociological or political situation or the workings of its constitution. Some countries have preserved a monarchy; others prefer the republican system; some enjoy the undoubted advantage of a two-party system, others suffer from a plurality of parties. Nevertheless, and bearing in mind that each has its particular variations, the link between the duration of the government and the legislative body is common, by law or in practice, to all of them. The link between the Cabinet and the Assembly is so close that, in the case of unforeseen circumstances arising which seem likely to provoke a ministerial crisis, the executive, as well as the Assembly, can once again be subjected to the judgment of the electorate.

The simultaneous election of the Assembly and formation of a government, and the identity of their political orientation and probable duration, should be further emphasised by a 'majority agreement'. In the eyes of the people this agreement will seem to be the *raison d'être* and symbol of the association of the two powers.

When a government seeks election it does so on the basis of a precise, concrete parliamentary programme, made up of a list of the measures it intends to adopt and a schedule of the dates on which it proposes to carry them out. A vote of confidence implies approval of these proposals and a pledge by members of parliament to vote for them when the time comes, or even, should the government ask for them, to delegate the powers necessary to carry out the programme.

A majority programme should be presented in such a way that the public can supervise its execution and penalise any failure on the part of the government or of the members of its parliamentary majority.

When a government outlines a policy in this way, declares exactly where it is going, and calls upon a majority for support, then Parliament should, and in fact does, follow. If a clash ensues in spite of this, then the President of the Council should have the right to dissolve the Assembly and allow the country to make a decision. This is logical since:

1 either the government has not fulfilled its pledges, or the Assembly wants to alter the terms of its undertakings; in either case it is natural to call upon the country to settle the dispute;

2 or the government is unable to reach an agreement with Parliament over some difficulty which could not have been foreseen when the programme was drawn up: then only the electorate can solve the problem.

These are the basic elements (a stable, assured government which is respected on this account; an Assembly with its normal powers and dignity restored to it; both subject to the sovereign power of the nation) of a workable system within the framework of the fundamental principles of democracy, and one which has proved satisfactory in all countries where parliamentary government functions effectively (*i.e.* in Great Britain, Belgium, the Netherlands, the Scandinavian countries, Canada, etc.).

The idea of a 'legislative government', however, arouses lively opposition among politicians who grew up under the Third and Fourth Republics and among eminent theorists of constitutional law.

Many of them believe that such a régime is only practicable

in countries like Great Britain, where tradition and social conditions have produced a political situation in which one of two parties is always in power. They claim that it would be altogether unsuitable to the conditions prevailing in France.

What basis is there for such a claim? Is there some profound connection between a predominance or monopoly of two political parties on the one hand, and a system of institutions such as a legislative government on the other?

The logical connection between the two concepts is anything but established. It is more likely to be a presidential constitution which necessitates a two party system. When the electorate is called upon to choose between two candidates at a presidential election, it is faced with a simple choice and can make a decision without much difficulty; a multiplicity of parties— one of the conditions of French political life—requires a more elaborate mechanism and the interposition of some inter-mediary body to constitute the executive power.

We seem to forget, too, that legislative government, with variations and in slightly different forms, is the rule in Belgium, Italy, the Netherlands, Denmark and other countries where three, four, five or six parties are engaged in the struggle for power. But it is somewhat rash to quote England as an example. The two party system is far from being a constant factor in British politics and coalition governments are by no means unknown in her parliamentary history*. From 1874 to 1922 the Irish Nationalist Party, with its twenty-four seats, was far from negligible as a parliamentary force. Nor did the Labour Party emerge all at once as a substitute for the Liberals: between 1910 and 1935 they figured alternately as the second and third largest party. And if by chance the Liberals are again in the ascendant, no one in England imagines the present system will collapse.

Finally, if one takes the trouble to dig a little below surface appearances, the fact emerges that when the political life of a

---

* Leaving aside the war years, there were coalitions from 1895 to 1905 and from 1931 to 1935.

country is monopolised by two major parties, this does not automatically obviate the divisions which, in other countries and other circumstances, would result in a multiplicity of parties. They subsist and appear within the parties themselves. Party discipline does not prevent internal splits and sniping, and even breakaways which may upset the party's majority.

Without underestimating the favourable conditions which England enjoys, it is by no means certain that the system of 'legislative government' is impracticable in a country which is not lucky enough to be divided into only two big political parties.

On the contrary, it is highly probable that such a system, with all its consequences, might compel the parties, or those of them at least which form the bulk of a parliamentary majority, to form a lasting coalition. Groups which have supported a government's actions in the Assembly and, to this end, have submitted to frequently painful discipline, and whose leaders know that the breaking of a signed contract can mean a dissolution are, in fact, bound by a much stronger and more honourable tie than were the temporary coalitions, combinations and groupings of related interests which have always been familiar in France. This is because they would not be combining for the sake of a piece of parliamentary arithmetic in order to achieve the mystic sum of three hundred and fourteen votes* but fighting a clearly-defined common battle on the basis of concrete commitments made clearly and publicly. When called upon to justify themselves to their constituents they would be compelled to unite again because, after working together in the government, sharing responsibilities and casting the same votes, they would have to defend their common policy to the electorate.

Thus and only thus, given the political situation and dominant problems of the time, can a broad group, or occasionally two, emerge in spite of the multiplicity of political parties.

---

* This was the majority required for the formation of a government under the Fourth Republic.

This is what happened as a result of Mac-Mahon's experiment*, an experiment whose bad reputation should not blind us to the fact that it achieved its object: it clarified an ambiguous situation by establishing two major coalitions, face to face with one another, and allowed the country to choose between them, in full knowledge of the facts.

In this way a system of legislative government encourages the formation of political blocs whose members have every incentive to loyalty and to ensure their continuity. It tends to reduce the large number of scattered parties.

The limited number of political groups, the existence of two, three or four major parties in a number of parliamentary countries, may well be a by-product of the workings of a legislative government, rather than a reason for it.

Fears and Criticisms

A number of French politicians and journalists have proposed several alterations and amendments to the idea of a legislative government.

1 Paul Reynaud and André Hauriou strongly advise substituting the automatic dissolution of Parliament in time of crisis for the right of dissolution at the discretion of the head of the government.

Rigid and absolute rules risk creating serious difficulties either in politics or in human relations. A constitution should leave to responsible statesmen the right of estimating the necessity for grave decisions according to the particular circumstances. There are cases in which the replacement of one government by another ought not necessarily to entail a general election. If the President of the Council retires for reasons of health, or commits some personal indiscretion

---

* In 1877, President Mac-Mahon dissolved the newly-elected Republican Parliament. Feeling ran high over the new elections. Gambetta urged Mac-Mahon to 'submit or resign before the sovereign will of the nation'. The Republican deputies were returned by a majority of 320 to 208 over the Conservatives. Mac-Mahon resigned.

which justifies his resignation, no basic revision of policy is called for. Indeed, in certain difficult situations a general election might well be a positive mistake*. In what may be a critical moment, the fate of the country should not depend on the blind play of insufficiently flexible machinery.

Those who believe in automatic dissolution do so on the assumption that governments would not have the strength to use the power to dissolve on their own responsibility and must be compelled to do so. They say that in the case of difficulty with the Assembly a head of government would renounce it in order to avoid upsetting the deputies and so lessening his own ultimate chances of a return to power. They go so far as to add that the Assembly would always be inclined to choose as President of the Council men whose character—or lack of it— would guarantee that it need never fear dissolution.

This is, to say the least, an arbitrary assumption and does not seem to be borne out by the facts. Things work out differently in countries similar to France, such as Belgium, the Netherlands, Denmark and Italy: there neither Parliament nor the government resorts to the trickery and fraud with which the French are threatened should this system be adopted. Moreover, the men who have played the chief parts in French parliamentary history would undoubtedly have resorted to dissolution, had they been able to, at the risk of upsetting the deputies and without consideration for their personal careers. Waldeck-Rousseau, Combes, Clemenceau, Caillaux, Poincaré and others during the Third Republic would have dissolved Parliament if circumstances had led them to consider it necessary. Millerand, Léon Blum and Tardieu at a later date, would have done the same. As much can be said for the leading politicians of the Fourth Republic: Guy Mollet, René Mayer, Pinay and Bidault.

---

* Eden had to leave the British Government in 1956, following the ill-fated Suez expedition, but this would hardly have been the moment to call a general election. The international (and national) situations were clearly against it.

My theory has been proved on two occasions and, oddly enough, by two men who are generally supposed to have preferred conciliation to an open breach, and parliamentary skill to harsher measures. Edgar Faure dissolved Parliament in 1955*; and Queuille, five years earlier, asked the Assembly to curtail Parliament's span. He fought to defend his policy and asked for a vote of confidence at the risk of losing power. In the end, a general election was held a year early at his request, which amounted to a dissolution. Many deputies must have lost their seats as a result, but the policy was forced through none the less. If the President of the Council had been able to exercise the right of dissolution at his own discretion, he would not have had to waste so much time or resort to such an elaborate approach and procedure.

It is clearly untrue to say that French politicians, unlike their foreign counterparts, would not use the right to dissolve parliament if it were given them.

All the same, we should not forget that conflicts between the government and the Assembly do not take place in camera. They are watched by the whole country. The audience is, in fact, the real hero of the drama. Public opinion, when it is roused to exert full pressure, will force a parliamentary crisis to a head to the precise extent that a majority agreement exists and everyone is aware of its terms. If it cannot do this, then it is right and proper that it should be the supreme arbiter between the two parties.

Clearly, then, the precautions which are being suggested to amend the procedure for dissolution are useless if not dangerous. Moreover, no necessity for them has appeared in other countries.

2 Other people take the contrary view and believe that dissolution should be made less easy and less frequent. They suggest that heads of government should have the right to dissolve only after two ministerial crises.

---

* The circumstances were trying and open to criticism, but that is another matter.

This was one of the restrictions which figured in the 1946 Constitution and it is one of the principal reasons why the stabilising influence of dissolution was missing from the Fourth Republic.

Is there any real reason why dissolving Parliament should be effective only on every other occasion? Either the system is valid and should work in all cases, or its disadvantages are too serious and it should be renounced altogether. There is no logical justification for the principle of alternation, making dissolution possible only in one crisis out of two. In any case, the result would no longer be a legislative government.

The most serious aspect of the proposal is that in practice it would deprive the first government formed after a general election of the right of dissolution. This would be the one which would have to carry out the reforms demanded by public opinion and spelled out in the programme approved by the electors. It must necessarily be a progressive, fighting government, facing up to a known opposition, and particularly in need of suitable weapons to accomplish its task. The French cabinets of 1924, 1932 and 1936 would not have been in a position to cope with their jobs more effectively than they did if they had had a system of 'alternate dissolution'. On the other hand, such a system would have worked to the advantage of the reactionary governments, such as those of 1925, 1933 and 1937, which marked a step backwards each time.

Lastly, at the first crisis the alternate system would encourage all the backstairs scheming we have already come across: nothing could prevent this, since there would be no fear of having to face the electorate once more. The result, instead of strengthening the executive, would be to weaken it still further.

For all these reasons, the right to go to the country in case of a major disagreement should not be given only to every other government. Every government, whether the first or the second since the election, should be able to resort to it in case of need.

3 There is certainly a risk that a head of government might

69

abuse his power of dissolving parliament. The fear of this haunted the Republican party during the Third Republic. Its members remembered Mac-Mahon's arbitrary behaviour in ordering fresh elections almost immediately after a general election had taken place; an act of real provocation to the country, which, moreover, rebounded against himself*. This incident is old history, but it remains as a warning in people's minds, and has made the principle of dissolution an unpopular one with many left-wingers.

To allay such persistent anxieties, it would suffice to stipulate that parliament could not be dissolved within a specified period after a general election. A limitation of this kind would remove any fear of abuse.

The President of the Republic

When Parliament and the government confront one another, each with its own prerogatives; when the National Assembly has the right to pass a vote of censure on the government, but the latter may, in the last resort, go to the country, then all the evidence suggests that it is necessary to have a higher authority to act as a guardian of the Constitution and a symbol of balance and control. This leads to the advisability of distinguishing between the part played by the chief of state and that played by the head of the government, and once again establishing the President of the Republic as someone without direct political responsibilities. This is the case in every other country with a parliamentary democracy.

During the Third and Fourth Republics, the chief of state was entrusted with only one effective political function, apart from his status as a representative. His was the choice of the head of the government, and even this choice was made in conjunction with Parliament. This arrangement should be preserved in order to prevent the appointment of prime ministers to be abandoned without any precautions against backstairs Parliamentary intrigues.

---

* See p. 66 footnote.

Such a measure would also reassure those who fear that conceding the right to dissolve the Assembly to the head of the government might result in the election of weak, compliant men as Presidents of the Council. They would not be chosen by the Assembly alone; and as an independent, permanently appointed figure, the President of the Republic would have a decisive voice in the matter.

The designation of a head of government by the chief of state and his final investiture by the Assembly would lead to ideal co-operation between the various state interests. This procedure would contribute to preserving the presidential authority and bring him personal prestige which would consolidate his position as supreme constitutional adviser. It is as an arbitrator on various occasions in the past that the President of the Republic has been extremely useful, perhaps precisely because his rôle as such is not particularly spectacular.

One Assembly, One Government and One Plan

Together, the foregoing proposals provide a suitable framework for the establishment of democratic planning. I shall examine democratic planning more fully later in this book*.

The development of economic planning should be based on the duration of the legislature. A year after its election, each Assembly should adopt a Plan, drawn up by the government, and should supervise its execution throughout its term of office. (In practice, the duration of the Plan would extend into the first year of the life of the succeeding legislature.) In this way a relationship would be established between the duration of the legislature, the government and the Plan. The government and the Assembly would know that they would be judged by the successes and failures of the Plan.

This would encourage candidates to emphasise their conceptions of the next Plan in their electoral campaigns, to propose their own amendments to it, and so forth†. It might help

* See Chapter Six, p. 87.
† See below, p. 101.

to clarify matters and make it easier for the public to follow the issues involved if, six months before the end of every term of office, the results and future prospects of the Plan were to be the subject of debates in both Assemblies*. Suggestions which emerged in the course of these debates would serve as a basis for programmes to be developed in the ensuing campaign*.

Naturally a scheme of this kind would not always work completely successfully. Unexpected events would occur to modify some of the facts: there would be government changes or reshuffles, adaptations of the Plan to meet altered circumstances, dissolutions of the Assembly and other factors. But it is important to try to keep to a rhythm as far as possible, and to get back to it when thrown out of step. The important thing is that the Assembly, the government and the Plan should always be associated in the public mind.

The importance of planning in a parliamentary democracy leads naturally to further modifications in the constitution of the government in order to allow economic matters to play a larger part in political life. This is the subject of the following chapters.

---

* See below, p. 101.

72

CHAPTER FIVE

POLITICAL AND ECONOMIC REPRESENTATION

HITHERTO I have talked about Parliament without attempting to go into precise details about its nature and composition. These are fundamental questions. There may be general agreement about the necessity for an assembly elected by universal suffrage, but the old debate still goes on about the usefulness of a second chamber. If there is to be a second chamber, people disagree about from where it should be recruited and what should be its functions and powers.

The Second Chamber

On the whole experience has not been favourable to single-chamber constitutions. A notorious example of their weaknesses is that of 1848 in France.

The advocates of two parliamentary chambers emphasise that laws cannot be made in a hurry. They demand mature consideration. A double scrutiny provides a check on precipitate or improvised action. The delays occasioned by two parliamentary debates and bills shuttling between the two chambers count against it. But the constitution can limit these delays and prevent the second chamber from wasting time and blocking the legislative's work.

The existence of two assemblies helps to maintain the vitally necessary balance of power. It helps to settle conflicts between Parliament and the executive.

It is relatively simple to work out a practical method of dealing with disagreements arising between the two houses of Parliament themselves. It should be based on the primacy of the nationally elected chamber and involve some mixed commission like that envisaged in the 1958 Constitution. (This proposal owes its inspiration to the provisions in the American Constitution for dealing with possible disputes between the United States Senate and the House of Representatives.)

Finally, and this is the most important point, in the past most reasonable objections to the Senate have been concerned with its method of recruitment rather than its actual existence. The system of dual representation used to be based on a National Assembly or Chamber of Deputies, on the one hand, which was principally the expression of political trends and parties, and, on the other, a Senate representing the various French *départements* but also, and this was its primary function, acting as a mouthpiece for rural districts and local dignitaries.

A system of the same kind could be used for quite different ends. All that is required is to apply it to today's more highly-developed situation. While a huge new area, a compound of social and economic conditions, has recently been added to the responsibilities of the state, the political parties have been witnessing the parallel growth of young democratic forces to interpret these conditions. If the electoral Assembly continues to express the conflicting ideological trends of the country as it has in the past, then the second Assembly should be chosen so that it represents these new forces: social groups and professional interests which the state must recognise as playing a part and having a right to participate in its workings*.

Democrats should not allow the transformation of the classical Senate to be an additional means of crippling Parliament and diminishing its position more effectively. For this reason it is only permissible if the National Assembly first

---

* Bertrand de Jouvenel has stressed the 'decline in geographical, compared to professional solidarity'. This development should be expressed by new institutions.

recovers its normal functions and powers. Suppressing the Senate which stands for local communities while keeping the nationally elected chamber in the position of humiliating inferiority that it occupies today would mean depriving the country altogether of an assembly capable of real, political action. The reforms outlined above are only possible if the National Assembly is a real political force.

These reforms are none the less bound to shock a number of traditionalist democrats*. But they must remember that in the twentieth century economics, production and distribution play an increasingly large part in government affairs. A Parliament of the classical type is ill-equipped to handle these things; it has a tendency to consider them in a purely political light and offers little resistance to pressure groups while the existence and functioning of a truly democratic power depends on a sufficient control of economic affairs.

For all these reasons it has become necessary to have a second Assembly, endowed with effective powers, incorporating social and professional groups, co-existing with an Assembly which expresses the nation's various ideological and political viewpoints.

In this way every individual is represented twice in different ways: first as a member of the electorate voting for the National Assembly which expresses his political preferences and ideals; and secondly, as a producer and consumer, through an economic council which includes the various classes, trades and professions of the country.

The facts which must be stated and, if necessary, opposed in order to reach high level decisions are no longer quite the same as those which set the tone in the last century. When people feared that government might become too centralised and that

---

* Also some French trades unionists who regard the state with a certain amount of mistrust and are suspicious of being caught up in a web of institutions in which they might lose their independence. Their fears are gone into more fully in Chapter Eight which deals with the place of trades unions in a modern state and a planned economy. See p. 131 *et seq.*

majority rule might become too powerful even perhaps arbitrary, they looked to parliamentary representation of geographical, historical and administrative units and to a conservative social structure to act as a counterweight. This was the original idea behind the Senate. Today, as yesterday, there is a need for decentralisation, but it must reflect the social and economic structure of the country and allow the forces of progress to make themselves heard in a forum shaped to fit these things.

This is, incontestably, a real need. The members of the Constituent Assembly in 1946 set up an Economic Council for the Fourth Republic and their successors in 1958 reconstructed this as the Social and Economic Council. The influence of the Council's work over the last fifteen years is positive. The value of this work is generally admitted—even though parliament and the governments of the Fourth and Fifth Republics have, for the most part, ignored it.

The main importance of such a forum lies in giving publicity to discussions of matters of general interest which are often little known and obscured by the intervention of pressure groups. This rôle of public informer and educator is in itself enough to justify the existence of a high economic assembly. It gives free speech to the representatives of the interested groups, allows the airing of minority views, and obliges every group to answer the objections and criticisms of other parties instead of being content merely to expound its own views. All these elements help to breed discussion and enlighten opinion in the country.

But experience shows (the Council of the Republic in the first period of the Fourth Republic is an example) that assemblies only play their part, only feel really responsible, and consequently only behave responsibly, to the extent that they participate truly and effectively in deciding policy. More often than not the members of a consultative body confine themselves to expressing the points of view of certain specific groups, and leave arbitration between conflicting ideas and interests to those

76

empowered to act. It is essential that the representatives of the various economic groups should not merely voice their constituents' grievances, however justified, but that they should also get used to weighing them against other claims. They should be learning to put opposing interests in the proper order of importance and take up a position on any given problem by first considering it from the point of view of the community as a whole.

A significant example of this is the debate by the Economic and Social Council of the Fourth Equipment Plan in 1962. Successive speakers mounted the platform to present the viewpoints of various specific organisations and particular sections of agriculture or industry. Each put forward the objections which, as he saw it, meant that the Plan offered insufficient advantages to his own constituents. The committee's spokesman (the *rapporteur*) stressed the basic merits of the Plan put forward by the government; then confirmed several important reservations already made by earlier speakers. His conclusions were passed by a large majority. But in the end it was hard to say whether the Economic Council had approved the government's original Plan or not.

From the moment that the Economic Council starts to take an active part in making and carrying out decisions, this will no longer happen. It will cease to be content with discreet reservations and pious hopes, but will accept its responsibilities in approving, amending or rejecting new proposals.

It is quite possible that it will reach this stage only by degrees, as it becomes fully aware of its position and influence. Gradually the views expressed will cease to be partial and specialised and become instead balanced judgments concerning the whole community. Then the Economic Council will be acting on a political level, in the highest sense of the word. Then it will be serving the nation as it should.

The Composition of the Economic Council

The working of the Social and Economic Council in its present

77

form underlines the need for adjustments in the representation of the groups of which it is made up; without these adjustments various trades unions and professional organisations, and also regional interests, will not be fairly represented.

The composition of the Council today actually favours the conservative, propertied classes at the expense of the workers and the forces of expansion, youth and progress. The present distribution of seats must be revised to ensure that the most productive elements in the nation are fairly represented. The need for a fluid policy of structural reform in the future means that we can no longer afford to discriminate against the very forces which contribute towards it.

This problem has been studied by a special sub-committee, set up with a view to arranging a conference to examine the problems of democratic planning (March 1962)*. Although no final conclusions have been published, it is fair to say that the majority of the sub-committee's members were in agreement about a number of principles. One cannot, of course, expect to arrive at the perfect solution to such a problem right away. The importance of various economic groups, the conditions in which their representation should be organised, the search for an acceptable balance between the consumers and the producers, who are in fact the same people expressing themselves on two different levels: these are problems which can only be solved gradually and, at least to begin with, by approximation.

After all, even the distribution of seats in the political assemblies has never been perfect. We are all familiar with the injustice which frequently reigns over the allocation of seats in the Senate between one *département* and the next, or of seats on the General Council† of a particular *département*. This situation is repeated in the National Assembly where regions with a high density of population are under-represented. Even with proportional representation, deputies with an electorate of ten thousand sit side by side with men representing ten times

---

* See p. 92.

† The French local council responsible for departmental affairs.

that number. It would be asking too much to try to achieve impeccably fair representation of producers and economic interests in the assembly in a moment.

Here the problem is complicated by the fact that we have to achieve representation based simultaneously on the following factors:

1 The number of people contained in each social and professional category (an application of the principle that all members of the community are equal);

2 The importance of each category in the economic life of the nation, as it appears in its effect on production.

Some members of the sub-committee already mentioned have suggested, in addition, that a third criterion should be taken into account. They call this responsibility, and its effect would be to increase the representation of the technicians and experts, of the employers, and of the nationalised industries (these being the basic industries which play a vital part in the economy).

To be sure the problem of emphasis is a delicate one; but this is no reason for refusing to face up to it and look for a better solution, although this may be reached only by a succession of approximations and by trial and error.

Consumer representation poses another problem. No organisation is generally agreed to be qualified to defend consumer interests at all levels, so we shall have to rely on existing groups. It is this situation which the sub-committee had in mind in differentiating between groups and associations comprising, on the one hand, non-specialised consumers (family organisations, co-operative societies, etc.) and, on the other, the specialised consumers such as houseowners (tenants' associations, and other similar groups), sports and leisure activities (sporting clubs, etc.), culture (cultural associations) and others.

Although organisations of this kind (and others which may emerge) are imperfectly representative, their spokesman might be admitted to membership of the Economic and Social Council if their numbers were limited to avoid upsetting the free play of the majority, and on the understanding that they would be granted a larger place when the consumers are better organised, as is the case in other countries.

A modern democracy is built up gradually, by easy stages, and its institutions can only emerge and start to function bit by bit. This is true whatever the conditions which produced the democracy; whether it occurred by gradual development or by leaps and bounds. Some form of initial compromise will have to be accepted, in the knowledge that the need for improvement will act as a spur to enable us to arrive at a more satisfactory balance.

Finally, it remains to settle how members of the Economic Council are to be selected. Should they be elected by the members of those social and professional categories in whose name they are to sit? Should they be chosen by the unions and existing organisations? Or could it be by a combination of these two principles: candidates nominated by representative groups to be elected by members of the various social and professional categories? (This is already the case in France in elections to organisations within the social security system.)

Personally I favour the third suggestion because it combines the choice of the electorate with investiture by the unions and responsible associations. Nevertheless, in order to facilitate the introduction of the new institutions, it might be preferable for the moment to have the members of the Economic Council designated by the various groups, as is the case today. This solution has the advantage of having been in practice for a number of years with satisfactory results.

If within the framework of democratic planning, we must come to some sort of quasi-agreement between all the parties involved, then the organisations which are effectively representative must take part, one way or the other, in choosing the men who will be responsible for the actions of the economic assembly; they must have a voice in the assembly in their own right. The result of direct elections without trades union or other group support (or, to an even greater extent nominations made, or influenced, by the government) would be to create two simultaneous kinds of representation while at the same time dissociating the unions and groups from active responsibility. This would result in continual rivalry and competition between these two kinds of representation.

This danger seems to justify retaining the methods of nomination which have worked satisfactorily since 1947 while reserving the right to look out for any alterations, improvements and adaptations which might become necessary in practice.

Furthermore, we have every right to hope that from the moment the Economic and Social Council enjoys wider responsibilities and takes its full part in deciding policy all the organisations involved will have an incentive to nominate their most representative leaders to it. This has not always been the case in the past. Of course each organisation would be free to nominate the delegates it thinks best, but I hope that, as far as possible, they will choose the ablest men and that the growing interest of the Council's work would lead such men to seek nomination. Ideally each union or organisation would divide the seats allotted to it between the various nuances inside it or specialised professions of which it is composed.

In addition to the delegations from economic and professional groups, another category must be represented: regional interests. If the Economic Assembly is to take account of the nation as a whole*, the Breton problem, or the problem of the South-West ought to find a hearing. This will not happen if its members represent only workers, employers, farmers and so on (the majority of them natives or residents of Paris).

In addition to adequate professional representation, the Economic Council must make room for geographical representation, which will give the provinces a chance to air their views.

This geographical representation should come from dele-

---

* And if we want to see a revival of democracy throughout the provinces. See Chapter Nine, p 151 *et seq.*

gates of the regional economic councils, which will be dealt with more fully elsewhere, or from a larger electoral body made up of the regional economic councils*, General Councils†, regional economic associations and so on, in proportions to be agreed upon, so that the region as a whole, rather than a throng of small subdivisions, is fully represented.

The Danger of the Corporate State

There may be some objections to the above proposals—as well as to some of those to come—on the grounds that they might lead to a corporate state.

But a corporate state is dangerous only if, on the one hand, professional associations are empowered to take decisions on their own authority which are binding on all those dependent on them or if on the other hand, institutional structures remain unchangeable, based on a particular, fixed state of affairs, while the economic facts themselves are changing. If this happens, particular or peripheral interests reap the benefits of disproportionate advantages or guarantees. Unless the necessary steps are taken, professional safeguards turn into conservatism and the only interests which profit are those contrary to the good of the community. For this reason we must draw our inspiration from the following principles:

1 Assuming that professional organisations tend to consider their own special problems in a one-sided and selfish way, it is essential never to allow them the power to legislate on their own. Let their delegates be heard, let them support the interests they have been put there to support, this is perfectly right and proper; but never allow specialised associations to take independent decisions (except occasionally in strict conformity with the terms of the Plan). All arbitration should be by the Economic Assembly as a whole, because in this way

* See p 153 *et seq*.

† *Conseil Général*, local bodies already existing (one for each French department).

the varied interests of which it is composed can exercise mutual control and hold the balance of power.

Some say that from time to time, interested groups would be tempted to resort to a certain amount of mutual 'backscratching'. Vine-growers, for instance, would help deep sea fishermen gain their point in return for promises of support in their own affairs. Combinations of this kind are bound to occur and are not peculiar to an Economic Council: similar bargaining takes place in the committees of the National Assembly or the Senate and even in the chambers themselves. In any case the risk is less in an Assembly of professionally qualified delegates (where everyone is in a position to estimate clearly both the advantages to be gained and the price that might have to be paid) than in a political assembly where motives are often purely electoral and tend to involve transactions which could damage the general interest.

Pressure by interested groups and lobbies will exist in the future as it has in the past. It is inevitable in a capitalist—and probably also in a socialist—society, because minority interests, legitimate or otherwise, will always try to protect themselves. The Economic Council will bring arguments and debates into the open whereas today they are carried on behind the scenes. Publicity is the best protection against backscratching.

2 Nevertheless, as a precaution against the risk of the excesses of a corporate state, the recruitment of the Economic Council should keep strictly in step with the fluctuations and developments of the national situation. It will therefore have to be revised at sufficiently frequent intervals—for instance after every census—for the groups to reflect correctly the relative importance of the various social and professional categories and their respective economic importance. A periodic adjustment of this kind will keep it flexible and progressive and avoid the dangers of age and conservatism.

3 Finally, in the event of disagreement between the Economic and Social Council and the National Assembly voted for by the people, the latter will always have the last word.

Indeed, it should be a stated principle that it is the Assembly which best expresses the general interest. The preferences of an assembly recruited basically from professional interests—respectable and legitimate, but inevitably biased—must in the last resort yield to the arbitration of an Assembly which stands for the nation as a whole.

The Powers of the Economic Council

With these reservations, the Economic and Social Council should become a completely responsible body, the second parliamentary assembly. No bill should become law unless it has passed through both houses.

The idea which immediately springs to mind is to confine its activities to economic and social matters, to the exclusion of political affairs. Such a suggestion is unworkable because in practice it would be impossible to distinguish between economic bills and those which are purely political. Suppose, for instance, we were concerned with the Common Market. This is a political problem of the first order, but it is clearly economic as well and it would be extremely strange if the Economic Council were not consulted. Voting the nation's defence budget implies economic consequences, and very serious ones since the resources set aside for military uses are deducted from other claims on the national income and inflict a corresponding reduction in investment or consumption. Other examples are numerous. There is, and in our day and age there can be, no boundary set between politics and economics.

The fact remains that the Economic Council cannot be obliged to pronounce judgment on matters which do not concern its members, or on which they do not feel qualified to speak. The following principles might therefore be accepted:

1 Government bills should be given a first reading by the Economic and Social Council before the National Assembly debates them whenever the government considers that they have a mainly economic and social bearing: i.e. the Plan, the budget, social laws, nationalisation, etc. The Council is also to

give a first reading to bills put forward by its own members.

After this the bills go before the National Assembly and in the event of disagreement the shuttle system outlined below comes into operation.

2 Other government bills and proposals tabled by members of the National Assembly are to be submitted first to the National Assembly and then, after approval, passed to the Economic Council. It is then up to the Council, in each case, to decide whether it need debate them. When it takes up a proposed law in this way it has the right to introduce amendments and modifications, and these can also be shuttled between the two houses.

Alternatively, if a bill approved by the National Assembly has not been considered (or amended) by the Economic Council within a given time, it becomes law.

3 When a bill is passed back and forth between the two houses, the last word is always with the National Assembly, according to a fixed procedure; for example, after a special committee made up of members of both assemblies has been set up (as is allowed for in certain cases under the 1958 Constitution).

These suggestions should satisfy both those who would like to see the Economic Council's legislative powers considerably increased, and those who mean to maintain the pre-eminence of the elected National Assembly under all circumstances, according to democratic tradition.

In a recent and much publicised article, Michel Debatisse* has outlined a theory which tallies closely with the one I have just described. In his view, 'the representatives of employees, employers and farmers should have an opportunity to reach agreement on objectives which affect their members' lives. It would be their business to plan the development and distribution of social welfare, and also to decide the proportion to be devoted to investment for production and for consumption. Even if it is understood that the last word always remains with

---

* General Secretary of the *Centre National des Jeunes Agriculteurs*. *L'Express*, 9 August 1962.

the elected chamber, this prospect still arouses an astonishing degree of opposition.'

The same author also demands 'the participation of economic groups, as representatives of the producers, in political decisions'.

CHAPTER SIX

ECONOMIC PLANNING
AND THE STATE

EVERYONE NOWADAYS recognises that the State is responsible for economic development. It is up to the State to combat crises and unemployment and to direct, stimulate and co-ordinate the national effort with a view to expansion and general progress. No longer can anyone sincerely defend nineteenth century orthodoxy or continue to believe in the validity of the old formula of *laissez faire—laissez passer*.

This has emerged very clearly in recent years. Moreover the majority of students have concluded that, in future, State intervention, which is already generally accepted in principle, should not take the form of a series of limited, specific decisions taken on the spur of the moment. It should constitute a coherent whole in which the various parts, instead of contradicting or cancelling one another out, as they have often done in the past, should be complementary and provide mutual support and reinforcement*. The Plan is this whole.

Whenever people are engaged in collective activities, such as

---

* 'The political authorities responsible for the common good cannot help but feel themselves committed to a course of action in the economic field which takes many different forms, is broader, deeper, more organic. . . . They have to act vigorously in order to give proper encouragement to the growth of production in terms of social progress and the welfare of every citizen. Their actions should provide guidance, stimulus, support and integration.' (Encyclical *Mater et Magistra*.)

fighting a battle, erecting a building or organising a private or publicly owned enterprise, they need a plan to determine the best way of doing it—otherwise the end product is waste and failure. The carrying out of the Plan in turn needs a fixed degree of power over men and materials—without this there is chaos and, again, ultimate failure.

Naturally such ideas are received with reserve and hesitation in right wing circles. They do not feel the need for a real programme of national economy; and there is still a good deal of distrust amongst them of the idea of interference by public authorities. Starting from the assumption that the existing state of affairs is the natural one, they do not set out to change it, but merely to manage it and to administer it empirically. Their concept of government is pragmatic, stabilising, tending to conservatism. The left, on the other hand, by refusing to resign itself to injustice or inequality, is always on the look-out for change. So long as dissatisfaction remains an emotional protest it can lead to incoherence and demagogy. Criticism must therefore be followed by the delineation of an effective policy. Today, more than ever, progressive men should be preparing precise, detailed programmes based simultaneously on the present situation and on the long term view.

The general trend of this economic policy is towards two objectives: raising the level of production and increasing the wealth of the nation on the one hand and ensuring a fairer distribution of that wealth on the other. Efforts must be made on two fronts simultaneously. This is why the Economic Plan must be complemented by a social one.

Historians a hundred years hence—even our own grown up sons in fifteen—will not judge us by any particular incident which makes headlines in the newspapers and induces the head of state to hold a referendum—but on the total volume of goods we have been able to produce, on the improved standards of living and on the increased opportunities we have been able to get for every member of society. The validity of a social and political system depends, as Bevan often said, on the

rhythm of growth which it is able to impose on the economy
and the use it makes of the surplus produce obtained to ensure
a more equitable distribution of material and cultural wealth.
This is the aim of the Plan, that is to say of the set of decisions
by which the community arrives at the aims it has chosen and
to which all must subscribe.

The first nation to organise itself on the lines of a planned
economy was the Soviet Union after the first World War. But
there is a vast difference—even a contrast—between planning
in a new, under-developed country and what can and should
be planned in one with a complex, highly-developed modern
economy.

The courses open to the Soviet Union in 1925 were simple,
basic and limited. It was a matter—as it still is in many under-
developed countries today—of restricting consumption sharply
in order to set free the greatest possible resources for investment and to give an almost absolute priority to basic investments. In other words, however hard to enforce, these
measures were theoretically simple, and it is easy to see that
they could have been conceived and drafted by a few, all-
powerful men empowered to frame a Plan which could be
made law for everybody. In a centralised, authoritarian system
the masses are simply told that they are taking part in a grand
design and are then mobilised to this end. They have no choice
but to do as they are told. The initial impulse always comes
from above. Moreover a simple, illiterate population, accustomed by tradition to obedience and never having enjoyed real
freedom, accepts orders and endures restrictions without argument. Elementary humanity hardly comes into the matter:
freedom, human independence, originality and even dignity
are cheap.

Freedom and Planning

In a highly developed modern economy the situation is very
different. Here, on the contrary, the organs of political power
acquire more numerous and varied functions every day. It is

89

impossible for the government to keep direct contact with the innumerable affairs needing decisions. Political power is exercised through a complex network of diversified bodies, social and economic organisations, more or less independent local or specialised authorities, banks, private businesses and publicly owned enterprises, trades unions, pressure groups and so on. There are countless decisions to be taken and any one of them may affect all the others. A complex economy means that policy must also be complex. The risks of error are multiplied. No handful of men, even if they possessed all the economic wisdom in the world, were perfectly informed and armed with the most detailed and exact statistics (which is certainly not always the case), could make all the decisions. At the same time, the people, having had a taste of freedom, want and need to understand and take part in the decisions made. It is not enough for them to see their lot gradually improving; they want to make a conscious contribution to a collective effort in the full knowledge of its aims, and reap the credit as well as the profit.

For this reason no planning programme in a highly developed economy can be kept in a strait-jacket of rigid centralisation. Inevitably there is more suppleness, more delegation of power. Recent developments in the Soviet Union show a tentative but significant movement towards this: centralisation has had to give way gradually; the rigid authoritarianism of the early years has become less imperative. There is still a long way to go but the direction in which things are moving is already clear enough for the unprejudiced observer to see.

If, at an advanced stage of economic and cultural development, powers of decision can no longer be concentrated in the hands of a small and selected group according to the totalitarian pattern, it is none the less true that an active, dynamic policy must, if it is to be successful, enjoy the greatest possible cooperation between all the productive elements of the nation. The fact that the men engaged in production are also citizens leads to the idea of a planned democracy in which the motive force, control and practical decisions, far from being the monopoly of a central authority, should come from the bottom. The sovereign power lies in the will of the people, and if this is to be effective it should not only decide the great national issues, but also intervene on all intermediary levels: in local government, regional sectors of the Plan, in co-operative ventures, trades unions and professional associations, business committees, etc. Only in this way will the planning authority be democratic at all levels and freedom, efficiency and social justice be reconciled and reunified.

Wherever a responsibility occurs, the appropriate mechanism must be put into operation to arrive at a democratic decision, by which I mean a decision taken with the assistance of all those concerned. The aim is for the greatest possible number of people, all over the country on the national as well as regional level, to play a part, consciously and of their own free will, in the organised professions and even in the business life of the nation*.

There is a difference of degree, and even in kind, between planning as we practise it today in France and the conception I have just put forward. At present the Plan is devised and carried out on the one hand by a bureaucracy which is, at best, neutral and on the other by groups who possess effective means of influencing decisions and protecting their own interests. Apart from some often purely formal participation from labour there is no democracy in French planning. Some day this could lead to disillusionment so deep that it might well build up a prejudice against the whole idea of planning. It is urgent, therefore, to correct this situation if we are to avoid the threat of future distrust.

We have seen† that the inability of the bottom levels of society to make themselves heard in politics does not necessarily prevent lack of firmness at the top. It is the same here. Professor Duverger is right when he reminds us that, where

---

* This assumes the existence of an organised working class. See Chapter Eight, p 131 *et seq.*
† See Chapter Two.

the State is weak, democratic planning 'is impossible. Even supposing anyone managed . . . to define the aims which conformed to the public interest, there would still be no means of achieving them. In a weak State, public administration (itself) is no more than an agglomeration of different branches, each pursuing its own goals, with no common direction. . . . The complicated apparatus of production is permeated by capitalist influences because the government is unable to impress its own influence upon it.'

A weak régime means wrecked planning.

On the other hand, a true democracy can inject new life into planning policy.

What are the methods of establishing such a democracy and ensuring that the Plan becomes something that belongs to the whole nation? It was the hope of an answer to this question which brought many people to the conference on democratic planning* held in Paris in March 1962. I have frequently drawn inspiration from these meetings in the pages which follow. They concluded that planning is democratic when it combines these conditions:

1 Democratic methods of planning: this means active participation by the citizens or their representatives in the initiation, execution and control of the Plan. In turn this means that they should be prepared for their tasks.

2 Democratic aims and goals: this means orientation of production so that it will satisfy social needs. In fact these needs are the outcome of two different preoccupations: the struggle against crisis and unemployment and the achievement

---

* This Conference was attended by representatives of the unions and political parties, students and politicians, under the chairmanship of the vice-president of the *Confédération Française de travailleurs chrétiens*, Monsieur Jeanson. It approved two important reports; one by Gilbert Mathieu (on social and institutional aspects of democratic planning) and one by Alexandre Verret (on the execution of the Plan and methods of financing it).

ECONOMIC PLANNING AND THE STATE

of selected aims. Both these preoccupations are clearly of prime importance*.

Keeping the Public Informed

'Freedom, in the 'sixties, means taking part in decisions.' The first demand of democratic planning, therefore, is that the citizens—or their representatives—should take an active part in the initiation, execution and control of the Plan.

Such participation implies a broad measure of agreement on the ends in view. But agreement is impossible or meaningless unless it results from the country in general being better informed: and in particular, those who are called upon to play a part in deciding upon and executing final policy.

Of all the great industrial nations France is, perhaps, the one where public opinion is least well informed about economic problems, although their solution is a matter of immediate concern to every family and every individual.

Schools and colleges allow children and young people to grow up in complete ignorance of these problems. Later on, having had little preparation for their rôle as citizens of a modern industrial country, they are subjected to the influence of the major channels of communication which disseminate official opinion at one moment and the opinion of private interests the next. As a result of this carefully fostered ignorance, and also of old national traditions (France has a century and a half of exclusively political battles behind her, while, in England for example, the important issues which have aroused public opinion have often had an economic basis), Frenchmen

* The *Confédération Générale du Travail—Force Ouvrière*, an important French Union, gave a definition of economic and social democracy in November 1961 which tallies closely with that outlined above. According to their definition, 'the following conditions should be combined:
1 real economic democracy at all levels,
2 a structure of efficient, democratic planning,
3 national administration must be adapted to this purpose.
However the economic aspect is purely a means, and the primary objectives of the Plan must be social.'

93

have reached the point of convincing themselves that matters of this kind are for experts only and much too complicated for the common run of mortals.

An immense effort is therefore necessary to raise the people's standard of economic and social education. The entire population has a right to be objectively informed about the problems of the Plan, the conditions of its success and the part that each man can play in it. This implies an entirely new conception of the press, radio and television in France: considerably more space could well be allocated to economic information. Likewise, economic education ought to begin in the primary schools.

Over and above the regular accounts of the Plan's progress, it will be necessary for the planning authorities and the ministers concerned to publish some kind of 'white paper' at frequent intervals to keep people abreast of certain major issues, such as building, land policies, alcoholism, agricultural exports, the motor industry and so on. Pamphlets of this kind, prepared with the help of workers', agricultural and employers' organisations and of the regional economic councils, could be a practical contribution towards forming the opinion which will be called upon to play its part in forwarding the biggest tasks of the Plan.

We must also start thinking now about educating all those who will have a personal part to play in working out the plan. Study-leave for the workers (with compensation for the working days lost) should become common practice; the educational rôle of the unions should be extended to cover simple explanations of the problems of industrial life and the way planning works; the efforts of the unions and all other groups and associations which are preparing people to take up their social and economic responsibilities should be given systematic support. When all these things are given the maximum encouragement, there will be a large number of people ready to take an active part in increasingly democratic planning.

Information of a kind is put out during an election campaign.

A statement describing the progress of the Plan and the problems arising from it should be presented to the public at the end of every Parliament's term of office. This document could then be debated by the National Assembly and by the Economic and Social Council immediately before the elections for the new Assembly*. It would provide the parties and their candidates with themes and material for argument in their electoral campaigns.

There may be objections that material and themes of this kind must inevitably be tendentious. It is a small risk if it makes the press, the candidates and their hecklers challenge statements, provide figures, criticise past behaviour and formulate suggestions and proposals for future programmes. A great step forward will have been achieved when debates of this kind are important factors in electoral campaigns*.

The Content of the Plan

The second aspect of planning lies in directing the economy towards two long-term objectives. These are:

1 to iron out irregularities and to fight depressions and recessions with the aim of making expansion and growth as rapid and regular as possible and eliminating periods of unemployment;

2 to exercise a clear, definite choice between the various social needs.

It is up to Parliament, as the democratic mouthpiece of the nation, to draw up an inventory of these needs, taking into account their respective priorities and the resources available, and on the basis of this to determine the targets to be reached by the Plan and the material and financial means to be put at its disposal.

This will immediately call for fundamental decisions concerning the rate of economic growth and the form it is to take, the importance of work and leisure, of consumption and in-

---

* See pp. 71 and 101.

vestment, the regional distribution of investment, and so on.

Every member of the public will, no doubt, have had to make up his mind on these issues during the previous electoral campaign, but the choice will still be difficult, even bitter. It means not only deciding the respective amounts to be allocated to consumption and investment, in other words to the present and the future, but making secondary divisions in both cases. In consumption this is between individual needs (food, clothing, holidays, etc.) and the needs of the community as a whole (schools, hospitals, old age pensions, development, ensuring equality of opportunity throughout the land, distributing income between social groups, defence, aid to under-developed countries, etc.). In investments it means discriminating between various types of production (some turning out durable goods such as housing, transport, etc.; others aiming at more long-term projects like engineering works, research, etc.).

All these decisions call for a deep concern with the public good. Such a spirit (the real community spirit) will only develop in men and women who are sincerely convinced not only that the choice rests with them but also that, once made, it will be adhered to without compromise: in short, who believe that the sacrifices they have agreed to make will have some meaning. The whole responsibility of Parliament and the government can, in the implementation of the Plan, be summed up as, a duty to be faithful to the will of the people, and to the contract they have made and a duty to be unyielding.

It is impossible to achieve all one would like to within a given period. The needs to be satisfied are always greater than the means. For this reason it is essential to utilise all the available resources, without loss or waste, and to ensure that they are used in the best possible way. No productive element should be allowed to remain idle or be used inefficiently. This is a policy of full employment.

The Plan means full employment placed at the service of democratically agreed objectives.

All the decisions taken and policies adopted which go to make up the Plan should be decided upon in this spirit. The result will be alterations and reforms affecting:

1 public administration and the branches concerned with it;

2 nationalised industries;

3 private enterprise;

4 financial concerns.

The remainder of this chapter will be devoted to issues involving the organisation and conduct of public administration. Relations between business and industry (whether public or private) and the Plan will be the subject of the following chapter.

After this I shall discuss a number of especially important extensions of planning as it affects the conduct and changing rôle of the trades unions (Chapter Eight) and as it affects regional life and economy (Chapter Nine).

The Plan is Compulsory to the State

One may argue about the degree of constraint exercised by the Plan over private enterprises; but where the State and its administration are concerned there can be no dispute. Strange though it may seem, it is not altogether pointless to mention this principle; it has never been truly respected in the past.

We are still tending to look for the best way to organise the State, its services, ministries and administration, in order to make the overall supremacy of the Plan respected. But this is not the important point. What matters is the spirit which dominates all economic policy and the concept of the Plan itself. No programme can be efficient unless all the men responsible for it, from the head of the government down to his lowest subordinate, are fiercely determined to be continually on the watch to see that every decision takes due account of the Plan. First of all, the Government and its leader must make the Plan their common objective, giving it top priority; they must feel that the Plan in course of completion is fully 'theirs', that they are committed to it and that it is on this Plan that they will be judged. If this is not the case failure is inevitable, whatever type of organisation there may be.

In times of war, everyone knows that defence needs take precedence over all others; every man at his post knows that his attitude must conform to the demands of the battle. The Plan should have the same precedence in time of peace.

Up to now, governments have not always recognised this precedence or been determined to ensure the success of the Plan even at the expense of other objectives (which are, by definition, less important, or they would have been included in the Plan). Time and again in the last fifteen years, a particular service or department, a minister, or Parliament itself, has taken decisions which, although individually justifiable within a given field, upset, and sometimes very seriously upset, the essential emphasis and priorities of the Plan*. Planning, in fact, can only be really fruitful when the prevailing conviction held everywhere, particularly by the head of the state, is the dominant theme and if all individual decisions should bow to it. That being so, no steps can even be considered in isolation but always in relation to the Plan in progress or the Plan in preparation.

It is none the less true that reforms are necessary if the administration of our economy is to function more efficiently. This was the intention which led to the passing, immediately after the Liberation, of the law of 23 November 1944: an initial

---

* To quote a recent example; it was unwarrantable that the atomic project at Pierrelatte should have been considered by the French government and by the National Assembly (though not by the Economic and Social Council, whose opinion was not sought), as a distinct, independent matter on which it was possible to decide without reference to the plan for the economy as a whole. An undertaking of such magnitude (considering the sums of money involved, and also the side effects in the use of experts and specialists, valuable raw materials, equipment, etc.) would be bound to upset the balance of the Plan and its chances of success if it were not properly incorporated in it (at the expense of some other project if need be).

attempt to secure the concentration of economic powers in the hands of a Minister of National Economy (or, as he would be called today, a Minister of Planning). This law remained a dead letter because the various ministries concerned (Finance, Agriculture, Industry and others) managed to evade the intended check on their activities.

The goal to be reached consists in reinforcing governmental unity by putting one man, (who might be the President of the Council, a Vice-President of the Council or the Minister of Planning,) in charge of all economic policy. He would be in charge of the Planning administration, the Treasury and the authorities responsible for the banking and credit policies and would exercise control over the activities of the other economic ministers. In order to ensure that these acted in a balanced and harmonious way, he would preside over an interministerial committee entitled to enquire into all important matters relating to each of these ministers as well as any business they had in common. He would be in control of the secretariat of this interministerial committee and all economic decisions would have to be ratified by him, as would decrees, orders and all important arbitration of the same kind.

It should also be understood that once the Plan had been adopted all subsequent decisions should conform to its demands throughout the period of its execution. The nation's annual budget, in particular, should set aside the necessary funds for carrying out the Plan. It is fantastic that when the Plan adopted in the spring of 1962 had provided for a calculated increase in the sum set aside for Education, for example, the corresponding amounts figured neither in the total accounts for 1962 nor in the budget for 1963.

In fact, once the Plan has been accepted, it should be possible to fix a great deal of the annual expenditure several years in advance. The sums that will be needed each year for work in progress, or already planned are not difficult to estimate—allowing for variations in the cost and other unexpected contingencies. Large sections of our finances can and should be allocated every few years, and would contribute to ensuring that work proceeded regularly and without interruption.

Finally, it is worth mentioning that all the principles I have suggested here would find very strong support in the reform of the Economic and Social Council described in Chapter Five, and also in the proposals I have to put forward in Chapter Eight on the subject of participation by the unions.

Drawing up the Plan

Assuming that political organisation and the principles by which planning is governed are in accordance with the foregoing suggestions, the Plan in future can be drawn up in several stages according to a fixed organic law.

These stages belong to two categories of decisions. In so far as they are concerned with fixing objectives and choosing a policy (consumption or investment, deciding on basic aims, etc.), these are political decisions which can be made only by the responsible State institutions. In so far as they are concerned with the ways and means of attaining these objectives and the conditions necessary to reach them, it is a matter for experts.

But the two fields are less distinct than one might expect. Some political aims and aspirations may be impossible in practice, and the statesmen who have to decide on them should be continually aware that they have to make allowances for facts, circumstances or technical objections. Conversely, advice by experts is not always completely unbiased. The way in which certain preliminary work has been carried out may affect subsequent decisions; alternative suggestions may lead to arguments; the way a question is put often reflects some unspoken assumptions. The politician must also bear in mind the passion, lack of understanding, and adverse criticism which may be aroused by the use of some technical methods.

As a result of all this, although at the outset the aims of the Plan have to be chosen by the political authorities, the elaboration of complicated decisions soon leads to a kind of shuttle service between the political authorities and the technical and professional bodies. This interchange should make it possible to arrive by degrees at a final draft.

1 The initial preparations for the Plan must be worked out by the Planning Commissioners. At this stage their concern is to assemble the necessary information about basic resources. But they also have to clarify the various lines along which the next Plan might be developed.

This preliminary work should be undertaken in close collaboration with the Economic and Social Council and the regional economic councils, which will be discussed further on*. It should begin two years before the end of the period covered by the preceding Plan (that is to say, one year before the end of the current legislature).

2 The information assembled in this way should throw light on the debate† to be opened about six months before the expiry of each term of office. Both houses should examine the results achieved by the Plan, the reasons for any defects and how they can be remedied, and the prospects for the next Plan.

Later on, at the time of the election, the same information will furnish material for campaign speeches and for discussions within the Parties, unions, etc. The best way of arousing the nation's interest in the Plan is to make it a major political issue†.

3 The new government formed after the elections writes a first draft of the Plan. It then puts its proposals to Parliament, choosing, in the light of the electoral debates and their results, between the various possibilities revealed by the work outlined above†. It may also, if it thinks fit, present a choice between two or three sets of proposals, with different possible variations in the rhythm of growth, more or less firm state control, and alternative aims.

These proposals are submitted to the Economic and Social Council and afterwards to the National Assembly who will take the general decisions as to the basic orientation of the Plan by choosing between the various alternatives put before them.

---

* See pp. 153 *et seq.*
† See pp. 71 and 72.

4 When the general lines have been laid down, they are formulated by the Planning administration, with the help of the committees on modernisation, the committees of the Economic and Social Council and of the regional economic councils. The text of the Plan which emerges is then ready for final submission to the Assemblies.

5 This text will be accompanied by several annexes going into details of certain aspects of the Plan: effects on national and local government budgets, nationalised corporations, the banking system, etc., as well as breaking down the Plan into 'regional plans' which will be discussed later on*.

All these documents will be put before the Economic and Social Council and then before the National Assembly which will finally vote the law containing the Plan.

6 The budget of the state will be accompanied each year by amendments setting forth any necessary measures to be taken to bring the Plan up to date.

Workers and employees organisations, agricultural associations, regional councils and the public as a whole will be kept fully informed at every stage of the proceedings just described. In return these organisations should be prepared to collaborate in rendering periodic accounts of the progress of various aspects of the Plan: regional, the different branches of industry (especially in the nationalised industries), etc.

In this way, the pattern moving from criticism of the Plan in progress to study of and preparation for future decisions and finally to the vote for the next Plan, should be succeeded by a series of contacts, or even exchanges between the government and ministries on the one hand, and Parliament, the qualified organisations and the country as a whole on the other. This will make it possible for public opinion and interested groups to be in a position to influence the general course of events.

It is the Assemblies' job to make this course clear and take the final, major decisions. Experts belonging to the committees

* See Chapter Nine, especially pp. 153-158.

and the government enter the circuit at various points to establish projects and amendments, forestall effects and formulate instructions and directions.

Under such conditions we may even hope to achieve something more than nation-wide agreement: we may arouse a powerful desire for the success of the Plan, a desire which will in itself be a decisive factor in its success.

Europe and the Plan

In these Common Market days we can hardly help considering an extension of the policy of economic planning into Europe.

How can France reconcile its planning decisions with its membership of an international organisation based on increasingly free movements of goods, labour and capital, and including countries which remain faithful, at least in principle, to non-intervention by the State in economic affairs?

One prime factor must be taken into consideration: in the world we live in, there are some issues too complex to be solved, some burdens too heavy to be shouldered, and some opportunities for development that cannot be fully exploited except by harnessing all our productive strength and to some extent pooling our resources and outlets.

There is no purely national solution to French agricultural problems. The remedies are largely bound up with the possibilities of exporting to our neighbours. In industry, the technical revolution in which modern nations are engaged adds to the cost and difficulty of social and economic progress if it is restricted to too narrow a geographical field. In the United States and the USSR, where export trade accounts for only three to five per cent of the national income, an enormous internal market exists for mass production. The European countries whose foreign trade amounts to from twenty to forty per cent of national production, cannot hope to expand on the basis of their own territory alone and must develop in step with each other.

National programmes for increased production sometimes

duplicate themselves. This is, or very soon will be, the case with the motor industry*, textiles, iron and steel, aircraft production, the chemical industries, synthetics and domestic appliances. Overproduction which is threatening to upset the balance of certain sectors of the economy in individual countries, may soon lead to an appalling waste of assets and resources, and mass unemployment in Europe as a whole, and to the failure of the Economic Community. At the same time other vast needs still remain unsatisfied within the Community itself.

There is no contradiction between national planning and membership of an international organisation which is pursuing a planned policy. The vice-president of the European Economic Community, Robert Marjolin, has confirmed this. On the contrary, it is hard to imagine how national planning would fit into a Common Market which renounced all official intervention and abandoned economic development entirely to the laws of supply and demand. In a situation of this kind, economic progress would tend to concentrate in the country which already possessed an advantage over the others in development†—and similarly in the most highly-developed regions of each country. If there were no control over random movements of goods, labour and capital, if all tariffs and restrictions on imports were simply removed, this would inevitably alter the whole perspective of the Plan of one or other of the States

---

* By 1970 European car production will have reached a capacity of eleven million vehicles a year, while the market will be able to absorb at the most only eight million. *Cahiers de la République*, No 32, special issue devoted to the problems of the motor industry in France and in Europe.

An important report by experts of the EEC, published after this book first came out, contained some extremely pessimistic conclusions. The report emphasised the fact that random investment has left the European motor industry wide open to the 'throat-cutting' already forecast by Monsieur Jeanneney, former French Minister for Industry.

† See the author's Speech to the National Assembly on 6 July 1957. Printed in the *Journal Officiel* 1957, No 70, *Assemblée Nationale*.

involved. All the planners' forecasts, calculations and general policies would rapidly become useless, unless the member States took the necessary concerted action—which would in itself constitute the beginning of supra-national programming. Pierre Pflimlin has gone so far as to write that 'planning on a purely national scale loses much of its effectiveness.'

Any nation must be aware, on becoming a member of an international organisation, that it is forfeiting some measure of independence and will eventually have to face up to fresh problems. It will be prepared to accept these restrictions and complications only if they do not mean changing or compromising the spirit in which it approaches its economic and social goals.

Democratic planning, as we see it, means distributing profits and investments in such a way that they benefit the entire community, and especially its most underprivileged sections. The Common Market could not interfere with these objectives without precipitating a grave political crisis. A united Europe, for Frenchmen, should not mean a Europe of trusts and cartels*, an organisation in which, at one moment, there is private agreement on prices, investments and production and on dividing up the markets—and the next, a self-destructive battle in which the workers and the consumers will be the ultimate victims.

To allow matters to go on unhindered in this way is allowing Europe to drift into a shape and balance which neither democrats nor socialists can accept. Europe, as they see it, should be equally opposed to any form of ruinous competition and to agreements which interfere with progress and the full employment of men and resources. It should not be a closed shop in

* This is a very real danger. The French National Employers' Organisation conducted an inquiry into manufacturers' agreements in the Europe of the Six. It appears that, between 1958 and 1961, more than 500 cartel agreements and 170 private investment contracts were made between one country and another (this takes no account of the agreements and investments involving America). The Executive of the Common Market has revealed that at the end of 1962 about 800 cartels existed in western Europe.

which every form of rivalry is allowed to run riot, but on the contrary, an institution which benefits one and all*. The only solution lies in planning for Europe as a whole. This will allow the member countries to develop their increased production in harmony without letting the elimination of protectionist policies aggravate the imbalance between highly-developed regions and those that are already depressed or threatened. Such a policy could guide the whole Community towards regular expansion.

Similar ideas on planning exist in most of the six member countries of the Common Market. Only Germany opposes a movement which, although still hesitant, is already wide-spread. Germany's scepticism and distrust springs from the influence of powerful industrialists who rely on their own dynamism to win new markets and do not want their freedom limited by national or international controls. None the less, they have been able to put their beliefs thus far into practice only because they have had the full support of the Federal Government under all circumstances; a support which has moreover, not always been strictly in accordance with economic liberalism. The Federal Government's so-called orthodox policy does in fact contain some notable departures and exceptions, such as those connected with and in favour of agriculture, housing, transport, energy, economic relations with Berlin, the development of the Eastern provinces, external trade, etc. Nor must we forget that German public investments represent forty per cent of the total national investment (even more if we

---

* 'Imagine for a moment that we were entering a period of depression. We should be all too likely to see the government of every nation reacting in its own way, extending the unemployment to its neighbours, resorting to intervention and protection which, though it might alleviate its own difficulties, would aggravate those of its neighbours. It is hard to see how the European Community would stand up to such a test. It is because the risk that the Community will disintegrate cannot be set on one side, that I believe, sooner or later, we shall have to have a European government able to conduct a European economic policy.' (Pierre Pflimlin.)

include military investments) and amount to almost double those of France.

At the present moment it is up to the Federal Government to decide whether Europe is to be allowed to develop towards collective planning, or whether it will retain a policy which in fact constitutes an obstruction to the aims of full employment and expansion in the member countries*.

It was because the problem presented itself in these terms from the very beginning that, in 1957, I deplored the conditions adopted in the Constitution of the Common Market, since these were 'liberal', capitalist and free-trading†. But Great Britain's application for membership brought a new chance. England is in the process of changing over to a planned economy. The Conservative government has recently come down in favour of a plan drawn up in collaboration with the unions. If some day, England, as I hope she will, becomes a member of the organisation, concern with expansion, full employment, social welfare, and democracy will be powerfully reinforced‡.

On 13 June 1962, the Trades Unions produced an interesting definition of their position with regard to the Common Market. They considered that the member States should undertake a policy of economic expansion and full employment, stimulate demand and the current of investment, and provide a professional environment in accordance with the needs of the economy. They expressed surprise at the Treaty of Rome's

---

* The theory and practice of planning have, after all, been accepted only very slowly in France (this goes a long way to explain the serious defects that still exist). Many people who opposed it ten or fifteen years ago have changed their minds as a result of experience and the initial results. We can and must encourage a similar development on the international scene.

† See the author's speech, op. cit.

‡ There is every indication that in the event of its being necessary to evolve a common economic policy, in the case of a world crisis, say, or in order to counteract the effects of an American slump, or to agree on new approaches to dealings with Africa, our views would coincide quite well with those of the British. This is less certain where Germany is concerned.

vagueness with regard to planning and State action where key industries were concerned (by nationalisation or any other methods). Another suggestion was the creation of a European Reserve Bank into which the member States would pour a quota of their resources in gold and currency to provide assistance for countries in difficulties. These proposals confirm the hope that a European planning policy would find support in England.

These questions are basically matters of political choice. If the Germans decided tomorrow to buy grain and meat from France in preference to Australian grain and meat from the Argentine, this could only be a major political choice. It is exactly the same with the scope of action to be taken by the Community to develop the west and south-west of France and southern Italy. The conception and pursuit of such a policy can only have political origins, since neither the technocrats, who are concerned exclusively with considerations of output and productivity, nor the representatives of private cartels, will be interested in the problems of reviving depressed areas or those threatened with depression*.

It is up to the parties of the left in Europe, including England of course, and also to the unions, to enlarge their

---

* In the absence of a European political organisation, decisions of a political nature will inevitably be made by existing institutions, even though these are purely bureaucratic or technological. M. Simon Nora, Director General of Economy and Power in the European Coal and Steel Commission, has recently brought up an important case which concerns fuel policies. Europe is at present faced with a difficult alternative. Either it must preserve, or even develop its local sources of supply, especially the coalfields, for political or military reasons, and by so doing increase the disparity between the price of fuel in Europe and that in the rest of the world's economies; or else it must accept technical developments and turn increasingly to cheaper sources of energy, such as oil today and atomic energy in the future. A collective choice of this kind cannot be left entirely to the existing European technological organisations; the diplomatic, military, economic and social aspects can only be debated by a European authority founded on a political and demo-cratic basis.

struggles for reform, full employment, planning and a fairer distribution of the national income, on to a European scale. If they can arouse widespread popular feeling they will advance together, and can influence the supra-national organisations.

The Europe we have to build is a Europe of democratic socialism, progress and peace.

To Plan is to Choose

The principles set down here which should guide the State where planning is concerned, have not been sufficiently in evidence over the past fifteen years. This is not so much through lack of technical means as a result of governmental narrow-mindedness and lukewarm determination.

The Plan resolves itself ultimately into a succession of reasoned choices. Because to govern means to choose, the Plan is first and foremost a political act or a set of political acts.

The ties linking the Plan to political institutions are obvious. And just as the Plan undergoes, in its choice of aims and the way they are attained, the influence of the political environment, and the inclinations and beliefs of the men responsible for it—so, inversely, the demands of the Plan, and the reactions and practices it sets up, will exercise a modifying influence on the workings of politics which is bound to have a positive effect.

I have said that planning cannot be successful in a State which is not both secure and democratic. But equally, a twentieth century State is always weak and incapable of fulfilling its proper function unless it ensures at the same time that economic expansion and social progress are planned efficiently.

CHAPTER SEVEN

PLANNING AND
PRODUCTIVE ENTERPRISES

LIAISON between the organisations responsible for the drafting of the Plan and its implementation on the one hand, and production on the other, poses delicate and complex problems. There can be no single formula for solving them because of the great diversity of the enterprises involved. Some have direct connections with the State, but their degree of dependence is in fact extremely variable; others belong to the sector of private enterprise but the degree to which they are independent is equally variable.

How will planning work with these enterprises, that is to say on the implementive level? This is the question we shall attempt to consider now, under three separate headings: nationalised industries, private enterprise, and methods of financing the Plan in both sectors.

I have divided these subjects into three headings for convenience. In fact all publicly owned corporations are carried on in what are still largely capitalist conditions. They feed private enterprises and, in their turn, are fed by them. All the time they are finding their own direction they are subject to private influences and pressures. Private firms, on the other hand, are gradually being drawn into a network of forecasts, controls and provisions which they may use to support themselves in the effort to adapt to present-day conditions, but which they may also try to evade.

110

This is the hinge on which relations between private enterprise and the State revolve, at the same time it is the connection between politics and economics. This area is difficult to define but rich in prospects, change and transformation; it is like a beach, dividing two quite different elements, yet allowing them to meet and mingle. It is also the battlefield on which the fight for democratic planning will be played out to a large extent.

The Nationalised Sector

The nationalised sector is, or should be, the privileged tool of planning*. Admittedly it covers only a section of the machinery of production (the total value of the principal public enterprises amounts to less than fifteen per cent of the French gross national output). But its overall effect and the certainty it gives to production as a whole that the set programmes will be rigorously carried out in full by public services and organisations, should be a decisive factor in the success of the economic plan.

The nationalised industries could play a considerable part in influencing techniques and economy by reason of their content, their share in the total national investment and the strategic position they occupy.

1 In France this influence extends over the following public industrial and commercial concerns:

(*a*) transport and communications: the railways, Air France, the Paris airports, the more important shipping companies, public transport in Paris, the postal and telegraphic services, etc.;

(*b*) fuel and power: the gas and electricity services, the Compagnie nationale du Rhône, coal mining, natural gases, atomic energy, the basic oil prospecting and research undertakings, and an important share of the refining industries;

---

* 'Economic growth implies expansion and direction of consumption and investment. Public control can facilitate both these things.' Pierre Bauchet.

(*c*) general manufacturing: Renault and its subsidiary SAVIEM (trucks), Sud-Aviation and its subsidiaries, Nord-Aviation, Frigeavia, etc., SNECMA (aircraft engines), Alsace Potassium, the Industrial nitrates, tobacco and match industries, etc.;

(*d*) insurance: the most important companies;

(*e*) information: the Agence française de Presse, a radio and television monopoly, SOFIRAD (with its decisive influence over the 'peripheral stations'), various sectors of the film industry, etc.;

(*f*) machine tool and supply industries, pilot agricultural enterprises, various laboratories and research institutes, advertising agencies, numerous activities related to public health and the social security system, etc.

This is an impressive list*. It will be added to later when we consider finance and banking†.

2 All these activities give rise to substantial investments. In 1959 fixed equipment and major upkeep expenses of the principal nationalised industries represented more than forty per cent of the gross capital investment in industry in the country.

* The constitution of the present nationalised sector has been principally conditioned by political chance, with the notable exception of the publicly owned banks and insurance companies and the big electricity trust. In some cases the object of nationalisation has been purely financial (tobacco, matches); in other cases it was a matter of refloating enterprises of considerable public utility which had been running at a loss and were sometimes on the brink of failure (railways, steamship companies, the Paris public transport system, etc.); in yet other cases the State wished to promote undertakings that were either non-profit making (Compagnie nationale du Rhône, Aéroport de Paris), or too risky (oil research); and in other cases again particular industries came under public control as a result of penal confiscation (Renault, etc.). This is the reason for the odd assortment of nationalised industries. Monopolies and competitive enterprises exist there side by side, some directed by their former heads, and others, on the contrary, controlled by teams motivated by a very different spirit. Clearly no wide conception of the use of nationalised industries could arise spontaneously from so heterogeneous a conglomeration.

† See p. 126.

It is quite certain that the enormous sums invested in the nationalised industries would never have been produced, much less put to effective use, if these industries had remained in private hands. The necessary capital could not have been raised or, if it had been (for example by subsidies or government loans), development programmes would have been dominated by frequently divergent individual considerations, and utterly at variance with the Plan for the economy of the country as a whole.

At the Liberation, there were one thousand one hundred and fifty private firms engaged in electricity production, transport and distribution. They were scattered at random throughout the country where chance or circumstances had put them, and they varied in size, efficiency and resources, from the small, isolated family business to the trust fund subscribed to by the most powerful groups in finance and industry. But for nationalisation, this heterogeneous network would have sprung up again unchanged after the war. Even supposing that each company had made, or received from the State the means to repair its losses and go on to more extensive investments, it would not have looked beyond purely local demands, or its own capitalist dealings with other firms, and short or fairly short term profit considerations. The country would have had no opportunity to profit from the pooling of resources which has fostered a brilliant policy of expansion, unified decisions, enlarged horizons and ultimately, to the construction, within a few years, of the system of pooled electricity which has given consumers in general the benefit of amazingly cheap rates compared with 1939.

Investment in public enterprise can lead to results of this kind in economic development and the achievement of national aims.

3 These investments have repercussions on the behaviour of suppliers and clients, whether direct or indirect, of public undertakings (concrete, engineering, electrical trades, etc.) and also on that of private firms who design their own programmes in connection with or under the influence of those

of nationalised industries. Here, too, public enterprise has a motivating influence capable of drawing the national economy after it. In this way, the EDF*, the collieries and the SNCF†, have compelled the heavy electrical industries to devote themselves to technical specialisation and scientific development which has allowed them to make up for lost ground.

For all these very real advantages and obvious opportunities, the experience of the last fifteen years, if not longer, shows that successive French governments have been either unable or unwilling to use the power they possessed (a power, moreover, reinforced by their right to recourse to numerous other methods of coercion). Governments have very often been either unable or unwilling to make public enterprises bow to their will. These enterprises have gone their own way, not wholly unsuccessfully in many cases, but without attempting to conform to the Plan‡. Not infrequently, indeed, it has been the nationalised industries which have set the example of indiscipline (where production schedules, investments, costs, wages, etc. were concerned).

Here are some examples:

1 The schedules kept by the arsenals and the navy in the years after the Liberation nearly always bettered the schedules laid down in the Plan and authorised by Parliament.

2 During the same period we needed tractors more than motor cars. But Renault factories preferred to turn out cars, and their representatives explained that they did not want to

---

* *Electricité de France*, the nationalised electricity concern.

† *Société Nationale des Chemins de Fer*, the nationalised railways.

‡ 'Nationalised firms pay more attention to the demands of the Market than to those of the Plan'. Pierre Bauchet, *Propriété publique et Planification* p.141. 'Every firm, even one run by the State, has a tendency to see only its own interests. . . . The economic calculations of a nationalised firm, if it is left to itself, make it take decisions which may improve its own prospects, but not necessarily those of the community. Certainly, it may be less concerned than its private counterpart about short term profits and more about long term growth. But . . . public enterprises, like independent ones, tend to confuse their own ends with the good of the nation'. *Ibid.* p.219-220.

leave the market entirely in the hands of their private competitors. The argument was worthless since at the time the State was responsible for steel allocations and so could easily have controlled motor car production by either public or private firms.

3 The nationalised banks went about their business with the sole concern of making money, refusing to grant loans to any business which did not fulfil the classic conditions laid down in orthodox nineteenth century banking circles; and indeed, frequently refusing their support to activities which the Plan was designed to promote.

4 In 1959, 1960 and 1961, during what claimed to be a strong régime, we saw one State industry, the Compagnie française des Pétroles, openly defy government instructions regarding Saharan oil, so successfully that in the end the government had to create a new company, the Union Générale des Pétroles, in order to achieve its purpose (perhaps one day this company will also decide to fix its own policy in defiance of the expressed wishes of the State).

There are many other fields in which nationalisation has not borne the fruit that was expected of it. Many people were hoping for a revolution in labour relations but despite some improvements (for example, in the rôle of shop stewards) there has been nothing of the kind. There has been no joint control, or even the beginning of a joint control which could have served as a test*. Doubtless the unions were not prepared; doubtless, too the technicians put in charge of nationalised firms had received no precise instructions and their training had not taught them to take the initiative in this way. But the fact remains that no interesting developments have emerged.

Nevertheless it would be unjust not to admit that several nationalised industries have shown real initiative in shaping original achievements: the 'Renault contract' is a good example.

* However, delegates from the employees do sit in the Administrative Council and play a significant part in the railways and aircraft industry.

115

In the majority of State undertakings, security of employment is surrounded by individual and collective guarantees* as also, to a lesser degree, is wage stability. The osmotic effect of these precedents on the private sector cannot be discounted.

The existence of state control in the basic industries has, however, greatly encouraged leanings towards technological development and modernisation. In more than one instance, state owned firms have been able to take on responsibilities, and even risks, which would have deterred private owners.

Altogether, as Pierre Bauchet writes: 'the cost they represented to the public, before nationalisation, has fallen, while the quality and quantity of services rendered has improved. But he quickly adds: 'Yet we have seen . . . how far actual policies still are from standards designed for the general good.'

It would be as well to bear in mind the following principles if we want planning to gain more from State undertakings in the future:

(a) A nationalised firm ought to be working systematically in the interests of the Plan all the time. The Plan is a major priority for it. The implications of this are, firstly, that the administration will not deny it the necessary decisions and financial support; and secondly, that such a firm will never hinder the execution of programmes which form part of the Plan, or attempt to deflect them into channels not laid down in the Plan.

Gilbert Mathieu says:

'It would be ridiculous to allow the present paradoxical situation to continue. Nationalised industries (banks, insurance companies, oil companies and so on) fail to carry out the Plan

---

* Collective guarantees give more security to the workers (in discipline, conditions of discharge, etc.), and recognition of the rôle of the unions. All the same, rigidity in the conditions governing some categories of employees does create a risk of bureaucracy and red tape which must be guarded against in the future.

On the other hand we know that wages have increased less in nationalised industries, on the whole, than in private enterprise.

or subordinate its requirements to their own secondary considerations.'

Alexandre Verret adds:

'For each nationalised industry the Plan lays down the yearly investment programme to be achieved; and their directors are responsible for seeing that the investment programme is carried out.'

In the past, nationalised industries have been subjected to innumerable strict, and occasionally niggling financial controls, but their economic decisions have been, to all intents and purposes, independent. There is no intention of impinging upon their essential freedom of action; on the contrary, it should be extended in many directions. But it is important to establish a regular organic connection between these industries and the Planning Authorities in order to ensure that their directors pay proper attention to the schedules and requirements of the Plan and give them absolute priority.

(*b*) One of their major tasks is concerned with the rehabilitation of depressed areas, or those which are on the brink of depression. The spectacular example of Decazeville has shown that they have not felt bound to intervene in this way. Although the closure of mines which were not paying their way had been foreseen ten or twelve years beforehand, there was no systematic attempt on the part of the nationalised collieries to provide work for the labour threatened with unemployment (they were even prevented by statute from doing so) and no new impetus was given to a notoriously under-privileged area.

In fact, if the development and decentralisation policies have hitherto produced mediocre results, the nationalised industries are largely responsible. Recently again, they have set a bad example to private enterprise by placing a great many new installations in zones which are already heavily industrialised, instead of in depressed areas. In Italy, State enterprises are compelled by law to sink at least forty per cent of their total investment in the south: a policy which has produced excellent results.

117

(c) The nationalised firms should show more initiative in the social field. The basis of such an action lies in enlarging the rôle of the *Comités d'Entreprises** (consisting of workers' and employers' representatives) recognising the factories' union branches, extending the system of paid leaves for study and training and, generally, keeping the unions better informed on technical and economic affairs.

(d) A reorganisation of the whole field of nationalisation is due, in order to remove the overlapping and contradictions which, while understandable in the light of history, have lost all justification.

It is not necessary for every nationalised bank to have branches in every *sous-préfecture* in France, in the small towns in most districts, and in every area of Paris. The administration has not yet succeeded in reducing the unnecessary branches, and it is time some general steps were taken towards eliminating the expensive and unprofitable duplication involved. There is no logical reason why the collieries should go on producing electricity in their own power houses when these should be returned to the nationalised electricity concern. Nor should the SNCF continue to run a fleet of ships in competition with the nationalised steamship companies.

Surely the State should be the first customer of its own businesses? What is the sense in the army buying trucks from private firms and not from those run by the State? Why does the State not set about the recovery of debts (including tax debts) through the nationalised banks in the cities, and through the *Crédit agricole* in the country? This would cut expenses and, at the same time, co-ordinate various activities and ensure a better general level of productivity.

The public, relying on tendentious propaganda, tends to think that nationalised firms benefit from important financial concessions, receive camouflaged subsidies, enjoy considerable tax relief, etc. The public would be surprised to hear that this

---

* See p. 129 and footnote and p. 147.

118

is the opposite of the truth. The State displays no favouritism towards those firms which are dependent on it for work and supplies.

(e) All the foregoing proposals, which form the basis of a consistent policy such as nationalisation has always lacked, would, if they were adopted, have a considerable effect on the general economy of the country, on territorial development and the extension of social welfare. They should be studied, defined and controlled by a specialised, high-level Council which would include representatives of public concerns, the Planning authorities, the unions, industrial utilities and consumers. The Council would be a useful factor in carrying out the Plan and would act, to some extent, as the conscience of the nationalised industries as a whole. It would be the expression of a profound unity, and would stamp its own approval to the scheme. Lastly, it could serve as a common administrative body: dealing with orders to private industries*, fixing wage and salary scales, and, among other things, putting decentralisation policies into operation.

Private Enterprise

The position of private enterprise in a planned economy raises problems, some of which are similar to those with which the nationalised industries have to contend. Other problems only affect private enterprises.

All the evidence suggests that for a long time yet, France will remain a mixed economy in which nationalisation and private enterprise coexist, both conforming to the planning requirements in a way that has still to be worked out.

Marxists have long believed that as the capitalist system matures it will lead to its own replacement by a new type of economy in which all the productive goods and means will return to the community. But our society has not developed

---

* A central organisation for government purchasing, such as exists in the United States, could play a very important rôle.

along these lines. Capitalism corresponds to no single model, fixed once and for all and incapable of alteration from within, whatever people in the last century may have believed. Capitalism today is quite different from capitalism as Karl Marx knew it. Its transformation is due to numerous factors: they include political democracy (which has had all kinds of repercussions on class relations), the growth of a nationalised sector within a still largely capitalist economy (a situation which Marx did not foresee), and the entrepreneur survival instinct, which has led to further and further modifications of some of his methods and practices. One of the most interesting changes is, in fact, this adaptation by private enterprise to planning.

In any event, the present work, which is devoted to more or less immediate problems, covers a period in which France will keep a composite economy.

In the nineteenth century, when democracy was limited to the political sphere, individual economic behaviour was still a matter of purely private concern which had no effect on public life. Democracy today is extending further and further into the economic field; modern socialism is, in fact, precisely this inclusion of spheres which were previously outside it, in the general fabric of democracy. Economic decisions depend less and less upon individual behaviour (more accurately, this dependence is in inverse ratio to the importance of the issues involved), and are becoming an increasingly integral part of the life of society as a whole. Conversely, there is a constant risk that political orientations will be forced on the government by economic facts or actions still beyond their competence, but which everyone now realises that it is the State's duty to control.

The experience of planning in France, whatever its imperfections, has shown that the means already exist of allowing its influence to reach and control spheres of production still legally in private hands. These means could have been employed a great deal more firmly and coherently.

To begin with, the very fact that the Plan brings into focus more or less certain prospects for a given period* cannot help but affect the manufacturers' decisions and plans. Some of them, assured of a market by the Plan, will be encouraged to invest in undertakings they would not otherwise have risked; while others on the contrary, will abandon schemes which the Plan has shown to be dangerous or unrealistic. Thanks to the Plan, all individual producers will have a better understanding of the economy, its possibilities and its ultimate aims. This informative aspect is a powerful lever in itself—and the one, in fact, which has had the greatest influence on manufacturers' decisions and undertakings over the past fifteen years.

There are many others: the governmental action upon currency, a qualitative and quantitative distribution of credit, loans at reduced rates of interest, subsidies, tax relief, various guarantees provided by the State, public orders and contracts, aids to exports, etc. All these methods have shown their real usefulness in making contractors conform to the directions of the Plan in their production and conduct.

It is the credit policy, without a doubt, which represents the State's most effective weapon, and this will be studied in greater detail later on. Any enterprise (private or public), finding its investment programme directed and channelled (by the control of share issues on the market, of bank loans and of self-financed investments) cannot in practice go against the intentions of the Plan. To be certain this is the case, clear rules should be laid down from time to time in order to make sure that the supremacy of the economic policy fixed by the Plan prevails in all circumstances on the marketing and banking activities†.

Admittedly the Plan cannot exercise the overall authority over private enterprise that it can over the public utilities and nationalised industries; but its influence can and must be

---

* If the Plan is compulsory for the State and the nationalised industries, its decisions over a given period can surely be anticipated by private enterprise.

† See p. 126 *et seq.*

increased, especially in the major firms, the industries which are highly concentrated and those which initiate production processes and which feed them.

Consequently it is important that businesses belonging to these categories should be required to draw up provisional development plans in advance and communicate them to the Planning authorities. It will then be possible to tell whether the total projected investment and production lies above or below the national goal; in the case of excess or duplication the authorities could arbitrate; in case of deficiencies they could propose steps designed to reach the goal. Equally, they should be able to satisfy themselves that the major undertakings necessary to carry out the Plan are put into operation—and also that, should it be required, firms will abandon schemes which do not fit in with it.

In fields where private initiative is still unforthcoming and inadequate to take the action needed to fulfil the Plan (installing factories in depressed or under-developed areas, for example), the State itself will set up centres of production and action, as it does in Italy.

Besides its methods of persuasion, the State could also resort to dissuasion. In addition to the positive, stimulating ways it can act there are also negative actions: sanctions and penalties such as surtaxes, the removal of certain privileges, selective credit restrictions or prohibition pure and simple. Faced with lack of co-operation, or by persistent apathy, it should not hesitate to use such methods.

In the event of serious and prolonged clashes between the Plan and any business or sphere of production, when firms offer protracted resistance to the realisation of a programme, or come to agreements among themselves which have the effect of impeding its execution, the public interest must prevail whatever the opposition. In the last resort the State can always fall back on nationalisation.

In a study of these problems the members of the Jean-Moulin Club came to the conclusion that it is necessary to nationalise any monopoly or any branch of industry which presents a dead weight of opposition to the State's planning policy. They go even further and suggest the nationalisation of given new sectors such as transport. Finally they advocate the creation of State enterprises when private initiative is clearly inadequate to meet the undoubted need. This is frequently the case in the economically depressed areas where private enterprise has failed to act despite any amount of official encouragement (Decazeville, for instance). But the Jean-Moulin Club does not see nationalisation as an end in itself but as the means of ensuring real planning*.

Gilbert Mathieu, at the Conference on Democratic Planning, proposed 'the nationalisation of large scale firms which systematically opposed the fulfilment of the Plan . . . and likewise the creation of public enterprises in default of private initiative'. The final resolution supported 'the extension of nationalisation . . . especially where a small number of firms achieving a dominant position in a key sector, show monopolistic tendencies and threaten the Plan, by ignoring existing regulations and incentives'.

A whole school of contemporary economic thought makes the objects pursued its prime consideration and regards nationalisation as no more than one of the ways in which they may be achieved.

Bevan, too, believed that all action ought to be conditioned by fixed goals. But in order to ensure that all aspects of production would be geared to the service of these goals, he laid down that the 'commanding heights of the economy' should be converted to public ownership in any case. Furthermore the criteria by which these 'commanding heights' should be judged are not invariable; certain aspects of the economy might be decisively important or not, according to circumstances. Fifty or sixty years ago no one would have thought of nationalising uranium.

---

* Similar views are put forward by Georges Boris in *Les Cahiers de la République*, No 16.

The extent of publicly owned enterprise in any given country and at any one particular time is not governed by immutable laws but by the prevailing situation, the tasks to be achieved and the degree of co-operation met with by the authorities.

The main thing is that the State should be certain that, when it wishes to develop a particular sector of industry, speed up mechanisation, prevent exploitation of workers or consumers, or, in short, to achieve any objective fixed by properly democratic authorities, it will be obeyed. What really matters is not the knowledge that a particular industry is publicly owned, but whether or not it will fulfil the tasks assigned to it.

Here a distinction emerges between the ownership of a business and the policy it pursues. This distinction is connected with the split which is slowly coming about between the capitalists and the proprietors on the one hand, and the technicians, the management and those who take the decisions on the other. There is a tendency for the major part to be played by the man who knows the job and not, as used to be the case, by the man who owns the property and the money. The direction of major private concerns—like that of administrative departments and public undertakings—belongs increasingly to the holders of diplomas and less and less to the shareholders. The engineer carries more weight than the shareholder, and sometimes more even than the man who holds the bulk of the shares. André Philip writes: 'What matters today is not property but the power of decision which is gradually becoming divorced from it'.

This differentiation is far from universal and absolute, and we must not make the mistake some do and believe that the capitalist class is breaking up or even 'melting away'. Many managers come from this class, or are becoming integrated into it and more or less consciously adopting the proprietary attitude of mind. 'It would be unfortunate if, in claiming to bring the analysis of capitalist structures up to date . . . we were to overestimate the incidence of a divorce between control and ownership'. (Bernard Cazes).

It is none the less true that their training instils the pre-occupations and reflexes they need into the technicians. Because they are concerned about expansion and productivity, they: 'have a greater tendency than proprietors and financiers to develop technical progress and capacity. For an equivalent amount of business and gross profit the former would invest more than the latter, and it is the latter, who, in so far as they still play a part in directing affairs, choose security rather than new plant installations. They are more aware of the legal, personal and financial obstacles which stand in the way of specialisation and less anxious for technical progress than their staffs*'.

The importance of this new class, about which Burnham may perhaps have drawn somewhat exaggerated conclusions but which justifiably attracted the attention of Léon Blum, should make co-operation between private enterprise and the public services responsible for planning easier than in the past and breed less suspicion†.

The creation of an élite of administrators and indispensable technicians is not, however, without its own risks The administrator's passion for efficiency can sometimes blind him to the human side of a problem and he may develop a real power complex. The possibility that the administrators‡ may evolve a caste system and an oligarchy of their own must be guarded against.

This is an additional reason for promoting the growth and strengthening, inside industry itself, of wheels and mechanisms which encourage the workers to increased participation. In relations between the planning authorities and the industries

---

* Pierre Bauchet: *Ibid*, p.243.

† Cf. Georges Boris, *Les Cahiers de la République* No 16.

‡ Sometimes in conjunction with higher civil servants with the same social or academic background.

there should always be scope for the working class and its representatives to play an active part*.

Financing the Plan

Manipulation of credit and general financial means constitutes the most effective form of pressure in the development of productive enterprises, whether nationalised or privately owned. In any situation, the control of credit and the finance necessary for investment can guarantee that firms will behave in a way that conforms to the directives of the Plan. Conversely, planning is useless if credit is handed out in such a way as to enable firms to draw up and carry out development schemes without taking any notice of the Plan.

Hitherto French governments have not used this decisive instrument seriously, although they possess the most powerful banking and financial network. Besides the Banque de France, the keystone of the whole financial edifice, the State controls the four principal joint stock banks (which represent fifty-five per cent of the banking activity of the country), *chéques postaux*, which is the most important deposit bank in the country, the *Crédit populaire*, the *Crédit agricole*, the *Caisse des Dépôts et Consignations*, the Savings Banks, the *Crédit National*, the land bank, (*Crédit Foncier*), the *Banque nationale française du Commerce extérieur*, and the major insurance companies (which are, in fact, investment societies), as well as their numerous subsidiaries. Lastly, the State exercises rights of inspection and control over private banks and can go as far as to veto activities of which it disapproves.

People at congresses and conferences call for 'nationalisation of banking', but this means one thing only: hitherto the State has not made full use of the powerful weapons it holds.

Mostly, the State has left the financial organisations of which, in theory, it is the master, to behave exactly as the old banks would have done before nationalisation. The problem here,

---

* These problems will be gone into at greater length in Chapter Eight, p. 131 *et seq.*

therefore, is not so much a structural one, as one of command and State authority.

The best proof that French governments have never had the will to use the means which, at least in principle, they possessed, is that they have never set up a general banking and credit managing authority inside the Ministry of Finance and Economic Affairs. Such an authority co-ordinate all financial policies and operations. On all the issues discussed in the present chapter, it should be able to give the banks precise instructions and see that they are carried out. It would not, as is the case today, give them purely in the light of circumstances or economic conjuncture, but relate them to the provisions and requirements of the Plan. Short or medium term credits, investment loans, evaluations of the resources of private investments, control of the financial market—all these things would then be supervised constantly. Thus a monetary policy—the complement to an economic policy—would be worked out at regular intervals.

To be sure the necessary directives would be brought to bear on general monetary policy in the first place, that is to say on the bulk of money and credit*. But they would be supplemented by precise qualitative details, aimed at public and private enterprises, concerning the investments advocated by the Plan and the criteria by which credit concessions are based. There has never been any attempt to organise the direction of credit in such a systematic way and hitherto no one has provided the banks with any criteria for selection between the various branches of production or of choosing the right creditors inside those branches.

Credit concessions should be made to conform to the projected Plan, and not simply judged on the financial profit involved. Banks, whether nationalised or not, have a tendency to connect loans too closely with the immediate security offered

---

* It is fashionable to express great scepticism about the effectiveness of monetary policies. But because it was formerly wrongly regarded as a panacea, there is no need to go to the opposite extreme.

127

by the borrowers. Such security should not be a sufficient inducement unless there is agreement between the projected undertakings and the provisions of the Plan. On the other hand it is no good expecting a bank to give financial support to businesses which, it fears, are insufficiently secure. In certain cases, therefore, the State must take a share of the financial responsibility, must guarantee the loan, or offer interest rebates or some other financial advantage to compensate for the risks taken in the interests of the Plan.

Under such conditions, both public and private banks could fall in with the financial programmes which should accompany the Plan. The way these programmes are presented should also be improved to make the financial needs of the different sectors clearer, to define the methods needed to satisfy them (bank loans, share issues, etc.) and take account of the borrower's own resources.

At the present moment no such scheme is practicable since the financial aspects of the Plan are insufficiently developed. It gives a good indication of the prospects for the growth of the principal industries but fails to provide those who make the loans with any basis for estimating which undertakings should or should not benefit from their assistance. In fact, as the Plan envisages increased production in practically every sphere (although in very different proportions), banking houses have a tendency to regard all requests made to them with a favourable eye, with the traditional reservations about security, profitable returns which have no economic significance.

The prospects outlined in the Plan for each of the major branches of industry should be accompanied by fuller indications of the criteria for granting credit facilities. In each sector it should describe the type of undertaking to be encouraged (structure, size, proportion of output intended for export, optimum relation between capital and turnover, etc.). Descriptions of this kind would allow bankers faced by extensive requests for loans to make technological and economic investigations and reach their decisions in a way that fits the needs of the Plan*.

In some cases businesses which were quite solvent would be refused new or increased loans as a result. In others the possibilities of obtaining credit will be found to be far from exhausted. If this is the case banks should use their influence to persuade businesses to widen their horizons. If this fails, the State has the incentives and stimuli already described.

Effective methods of action would include the reform of the *Bourse* regulating the market by means of a capital gains tax, and the establishment of scheduled share issues (which would benefit both nationalised industries and private enterprise) in accordance with the needs of the Plan.

Another set of questions which are more important still, concern the relation of planning to reinvested profits (self-financing). There is much to be said on both sides about this method of business finance. In all modern nations—the Soviet Union as well as the United States, in Germany and in France —public or private undertakings are increasingly finding an important part of the resources they need for machinery, equipment and modernisation by adding a supplementary profit margin to their prices. A watch must be kept on the disadvantages of this and for the abuses and disorganisation it can cause, as well as the deviations from the Plan which it may encourage by allowing useless and inopportune or selfish investments whose cost has still to be borne by the consumer, in other words, by the community as a whole. For this reason it is vital to make arrangements whereby the capital raised by

---

* They will be equally indispensable in enlightening the *Comités d'Entreprises* (set up in France by legislation and where the workers' elected representatives and the employers discuss matters of common interest) and give them an idea of the kind of development or conversion that should be introduced in the interests of the Plan. Information of this kind will be of much more use to the *Comités* than the limited and purely economic information given in the present Plan and which cannot be translated into terms appropriate to the life of any one particular business.

E

this profit margin can be put to some use which helps the Plan and deflected from those at odds with it*.

Directing all efforts towards a Common Goal

The Plan must have the support of everyone: the President of the Council in his office, the research worker in his laboratory, and the worker in his factory. But agriculture and industry clearly play a decisive part in the realisation of the Plan. 'No economic system has ever succeeded in replacing the responsibility of the directors of enterprises. On the contrary, the pursuit of ambitious aims presupposes universal energy and initiative'. (Alexandre Verret). Enterprise represents the stage of implementation and execution without which the preliminary work, discussions, and decision-making would be so much wind.

A contrast is sometimes, unnecessarily, drawn between private and public enterprise. 'There is no series of autonomous acts, separate and unconnected, which correspond . . . to their division'. (François Bloch-Lainé). Everything, in both cases, should tend towards a common goal.

In this sense every business is a public service and the Plan is something which belongs to the whole nation.

---

* Alexandre Verret, in the report I have already quoted, has proposed a system of calculating the 'Plan margin' in every sphere, with the object of allowing businesses the facilities of profit margins, in proportion to their needs, but so that the amount of credit would be known and its use subject to control. This system could easily be applied to nationalised industries, and possibly also to the larger private enterprises; other methods would have to be found for less important firms.

During the war the Vichy government, at the instigation of the occupation authorities, set up a very efficient system to make sure that profit margins were used in a way that coincided with the needs of the German war effort. What worked effectively 'for the king of Prussia' can be used with as much success tomorrow in the national interest.

130

CHAPTER EIGHT

PROMOTING
TRADES UNIONS

THE RÔLE of the trades unions is continually increasing and their scope growing wider. It is worth considering the implications for them of the establishment of the Economic and Social Council and the regional economic councils (the setting up of which will be discussed later*), since the unions must be strongly represented in both these organisations.

Unions will certainly remain absolutely independent of the State and continue as the natural defenders of the workers' claims. Nevertheless, their participation in economic discussions and decisions on a national and regional level—an essential for the establishment of a modern democratic society —will bring them new responsibilities.

Opponents of this development often base their objections on the fact that the unions are insufficiently representative, since in fact only a small proportion of workers in France belong to a union. But their influence spreads far beyond the fraction who pay their subscriptions and may be seen as a series of concentric circles whose radius extends over the different layers of the working class. In the centre is a solid kernel made up of the moving forces, secretaries and shop stewards who keep the sections alive, agitate and turn up at private meetings as well as public demonstrations, and who

---

* See Chapter Nine, especially p. 153 *et seq.*

are in constant touch with headquarters and almost always ready to do as they are told. In the next circle are those who, without being permanently or actively engaged in the fight, show their solidarity by going to the more important meetings and paying their dues fairly regularly. This section has grown not only in nationalised industries, but also in certain vital sectors concerned with the most modern and technically highly-developed industries, with a high degree of mechanisation and automation (such as oil, chemicals, electronics, etc., where the proportion of union membership in France often reaches as much as fifty per cent). Next come those who, although they take no official part in union activities, are in the habit of basing their personal behaviour on the directives of one or other organisation. These are irregular followers, admittedly, but the unions exercise a fairly strong influence over them none the less, especially under special circumstances. Lastly comes the lethargic and disorganised mass. Even those workers are not totally indifferent to the unions. Under exceptional circumstances the unions (if they choose their ground well) would probably be capable—in a strike for example—of rallying the almost unanimous support of the employees of any particular firm or industry. The unions' effectiveness, therefore, cannot be judged by the percentage of paid-up members among the workers, but rather by their ability to bring about a succession of direct or indirect actions. It would be wrong to underestimate them*.

This influence will increase as the unions find themselves in possession of fresh rights and fresh opportunities for action and participation. If the French farm workers' unions have managed to attract a considerable proportion of supporters in a very few years, it is because they have long been looked upon as having

---

* Sometimes, for instance, a branch of the CGT (*Confédération Général du Travail*, a large Communist controlled Union) which has only ten per cent of dues-paying members in a particular factory, gets fifty-five or sixty per cent of the votes when it comes to an election to the *Comités d'Entreprise*.

official status. Because of this the farmers have come to take an increasingly lively interest in their affairs, in the choice of leaders and the conduct of matters of general importance. The same will happen in the workers' unions as soon as their rôle in the State is organised on official lines.

The present chapter will be concerned with the place which the trades unions should occupy in the reformed State, their rôle in national planning (according to the proposals outlined in chapters five, six and seven), and the way in which relations between industry and the unions should be developed, in connection with the planning process (which was described in chapter seven). The rôle of the unions in the regional sphere will be considered in chapter nine.

Democratic Planning and the Unions

In a number of countries the unions exert their influence on public life mainly through the political parties. They formulate their claims—which are not necessarily confined to social problems—and compel a party either to support or oppose them. The unions and the parties are bound together in practice and sometimes in law. At times a party will try to gain control of a union, at least in matters unconnected with social claims. At others, a party seems to have become dependent on a union.

In France there have always been connections between certain union organisations and certain parties. But French unions have been more anxious to safeguard their independence than they have in other countries, not only from the political organisations but from political activity of any kind. The Charter of Amiens of 1905 is a categoric commitment to this end.

A fierce will to independence is the dominant psychological trait in many French union leaders. It operates, not only against management, whether private or public not only against the political parties, but also against the existing economic régime and against any future régime, even a socialist one. This breeds a profound distrust of any commitment which extends even to compulsory arbitration procedures (which a number of unions in other countries accept). It breeds, too, the will to maintain the right to strike in all circumstances, and a lively antagonism to any political system which would restrict this right (this is one of the obstacles encountered by Communist propaganda in eulogising the Iron Curtain systems which have abolished it).

Another consequence of the desire to see the unions remain totally free in the face of all social, economic or political forces is every worker's right to reject a particular union if he does not consider it sufficiently independent. This leads to the ever-present possibility of a multiplication of union organisations and the rejection of the single union which is considered by many French workers to be in danger of becoming either an official, State union or the mouthpiece of a particular party.

For the working class, and even for the community as a whole, divided unions have serious disadvantages: they encourage rivalry and ill-feeling and they lead to one union outbidding the other. But, in present day France, the disadvantages are inevitable. It is up to the unions, acting on democratic principles, to work out amongst themselves the means of co-operation, whether lasting or temporary, and whether they cover a broad or a narrow field. It would be out of the question to bring outside pressure to bear or to infringe union freedom. Their right to multiply is still the best guarantee of their independence. Furthermore, in the present state of French affairs, there are occasions when the co-operation of separate organisations confers on the workers a power and strength greatly superior to that which they would possess if they were forced into a single, artificial unit.

French workers' refusal to allow themselves to be organised into a monolithic body rests, in the last resort, on a profound instinct for democracy. Democracy is incompatible with compulsory integration; it acknowledges the diversity of groups and individuals and demands that freedom of choice shall be respected. Distrust for the Iron Curtain unions springs from this: there is a feeling that workers' organisations ought not to be put at the service of the State, even if many of their members believe it to be acting in the interests of the working class. Democratic socialism needs discussion and freedom of debate: whatever happens it must defend the right of all to challenge authority and official decisions. The unions need and mean to preserve the same rights.

Professor Maurice Hauriou has written: 'the only way any democracy survives is by a popular sense of self-preservation'. Trades unionism in a modern democratic state is animated by a similar spirit, one which Paul Vignaux, a French union official defined as: 'the spirit of any claim in which a self-respecting individual asserts his own rights as an individual or those of the community to which he belongs, and fights for their recognition, risking his goods, and sometimes his life in the struggle'. Trades unionism of this kind does not forget that there is always a conflict ahead, and that even in a nation founded on fundamentally socialist and egalitarian principles it will be a long time before the different elements of the population can exist in harmony, while it will always be necessary to keep a watch on the administration.

But there is one way in which the conflict can be resolved: it lies in transforming the organs of power in such a way that they will guarantee ample room for the will of the people. Then, once the inevitable clashes are over, there is a possibility of reaching agreements. The working class will naturally wish to have a say in these agreements through its own organisations, and to be able to discuss and even reject them. Moreover, because there should always be a way of expressing different points of view within the organisations themselves, there will still be room for separate unions to exist side by side—each representing a particular bias or tendency.

Having defined trades unionism as capable of free action and independent decisions, we must now examine the part it will play in a democratically planned economy. This cannot be

135

equated with the part it plays in a liberal capitalist economy or in a planned economy of a totalitarian type.

Trades union behaviour in a liberal economy, such as that of Great Britain or France a hundred years ago, for instance, is easily defined. The whole economic structure is based on the principle of *laissez faire*, *laissez passer*, and the law of the jungle operates. Economic development works in and through the struggle between the various productive forces, in other words between social classes. In order to win concessions, since the situation guarantees them no security, the workers form associations, even when these are forbidden, and fight for gradual recognition. They cannot rely on the State to bring about alterations and reforms, because the State is in the hands of other and dominant social forces. The rôle of the unions in such a situation is clearly a totally aggressive one. Using the weapons at their disposal such as strikes (whether legal or illegal) they aim no higher than conflicts and claims and bringing constant pressure to bear on the other parties to their disputes in the hope of making the distribution of the national income less unfair.

The situation is quite different under a régime where there is planning of an autocratic and dictatorial kind. Then the Plan is promulgated from above by an all-powerful centralised authority whose decisions are binding on everyone. Trades unions, like all other organisations and institutions, are compelled to bow before the Plan and carry it out. There is only room for one union in a system of this kind (or rather, if there were several, then the aims and objects of all of them would be identical), just as there is, in general, only one political party. Union, party and administration are all simply the instruments of the central power, there is no room for bargaining, disputes or opposition. The union merely applies decisions which have been taken elsewhere.

What will happen if we achieve democratic planning?

1 *In drawing up the Plan*. The presence of union representatives in the organisations where the Plan is drawn up and

ratified is the decisive factor in any system of democratisation. Without this, the Plan would not achieve the desired shape. It would remain bureaucratic and technocratic and subject to other influences with no democratic checks and balances. Before being accepted, this new concept of planning with union assistance will meet a good many obstacles; perhaps the most serious will be a psychological one. This obstacle lies in France in the union member's distrust of authority, mentioned elsewhere, and is based on a long history of social and economic injustice. Modern developments have modified the scope and severity of this injustice, but the workers are still profoundly affected by it in spirit and it must be borne in mind in any endeavour to introduce new methods of discussion, of argument and ultimately of co-operation.

To wipe out the effects of the past, and get the right degree of co-operation from the workers, they must first be guaranteed a stronger position.

At once this brings us back to the importance of spreading information about economic affairs. It is well known that the unions are unwilling to trust any figures put before them by the employers, the management or even the administration. It is vital that in the mixed committees there should be a constant comparison between official statements and statistics and those furnished by the labour organisations. When statistics are presented, the union representatives should know how they have been arrived at, on what basis and by what means, why and how any particular adjustment has been taken into consideration, and so on. The financial side of the economy, like the actual business of planning, should be carried on in a glass house. This is the only way in which to create the atmosphere of trust which alone can make any common achievement possible.

The terms of the discussion, even the actual words used, should be extensively revised. Too often, as one union official, Roger Jacques, has put it: 'militant trades unionists in mixed discussions have the feeling that they are the outsiders in a

E*

tight family circle'. So long as this attitude persists, and is fostered by some managers or employers, co-operation will have enormous obstacles to face.

The proportion of workers in the commissions is another important factor in breaking down their sense of isolation and the feeling of being insufficiently represented. At present they form not more than a tenth of the various Commissions in the French Planning Administration. The remaining ninety per cent is made up more or less equally by civil servants and representatives of the employers. This imbalance is a supplementary factor in creating unease and suspicion. It should, therefore, be corrected.

2 *In Controlling the Plan.* If, after the Plan has been drawn up, one or more unions disagree with the decisions that have been taken, if they feel that these do not give the working class a fair share of the national income, then they will automatically oppose the Plan. They will fight it with traditional means which nothing can check or remove.

If, on the other hand, the Plan receives their support, a new situation arises. The result might now be called a quasi-contract, in other words a certain measure of commitment. The unions still have the right to protest, but in this case it works very differently from the conditions prevailing in the capitalist economy of the nineteenth century.

Should the State or those responsible for production fail to fulfil their subsequent obligations, or try to elude the Plan's discipline, then the unions would be able to protest against the violation of the quasi-contract and take appropriate action. They are in a position, through the methods of protest and retaliation at their disposal, to enforce respect for their commitments on all who attempt to evade them.

For this to be possible they must be able to check on the behaviour of all those involved (and on that of the State in particular). It is therefore essential that they should have a say in the supervision of the execution of decisions taken with their approval. This leads to fresh responsibility, also bound up with the democratic nature of the Plan and with the quasi-contract which has been agreed upon. It is impossible to be a party to a contract and not claim the right and the means to determine the respect in which it is held by the other parties.

3 *In the execution of the Plan.* Assuming that all parties do their duty and behave in such a way as to make a success of the Plan, it follows that the unions ought also to make an active contribution, since this will be in the interest of their own members. It is no longer a question of preventing sabotage and cheating, but of collaborating in a collective effort towards a predetermined goal. A situation might arise in which the unions will be able to stimulate a particular official or sector of production whose lack of efficiency they have detected. This means positive action in the execution of the Plan and this is the third form which the union's assistance will take.

The nature and direction of union action is radically changed by the fact that democratic planning demands the co-operation of an organised working class. Once again, such planning is inconceivable unless the extension of the unions' rôle is accepted by the unions themselves.

We are no longer living in a liberal economy and we are moving further away from it every day. The workers' organisations have to reconcile the effects of this with their inalienable right to protest and make demands. They will have to revise their rules and principles in accordance with the changes that are taking place. This is the condition upon which the success of a democratic economy depends.

The rapid development of an industrial society involves a whole series of other problems concerning the number and organisation of the men who undertake the concrete tasks of planning. Democratic organisations in general and the trades unions in particular have still not got enough men at their disposal prepared to undertake a task whose scope is growing larger every day. But the fact that decisions will no longer be delegated to limited groups, but must be reached and enforced by a growing number of responsible men and qualified intermediaries, means that an economic democracy will need more and more of these competent people.

In the initial stages we must rely basically on men trained in and by action. We cannot wait to move forward until we have a sufficient number of utterly reliable and experienced social leaders. We must work with the means to hand, even if this leads to some initial problems. In the nineteenth century when universal suffrage was given to all citizens, not all of them were capable of making the best use of it. There were some then who maintained—apparently reasonably—that only those with a sufficiently high standard of education should be allowed to vote. But if political rights had been reserved for those able to read and write it seems likely that compulsory education would not have been introduced until perhaps a century later, and universal suffrage would have been delayed by the same length of time. It is better to take a few risks than to mark time. Today's situation is in many ways comparable. The present generation has to embark on economic democracy, even if everyone is not yet equipped to make the best decisions on such questions all the time.

This does not obviate the need, if economic action and planning are to succeed, for training the maximum number of men to shoulder their responsibilities. The technical, economic and even political evolution of the working population and their representatives is one of the major tasks before the democrats and trades unionists in European countries.

In fact real progress has already been made. The organisation of the workers, both regionally and in industry as a whole, shows that the leaders and active members of the unions have acquired a great deal of knowledge, empirically, in the past fifteen years. They can claim a good deal of credit for this, since it is a development which repression and obstruction of one kind or another have done much to hinder. Moreover such restrictions have been increasing in France in the past few years, because of the decline of political democracy and freedom. This is always accompanied by a recrudescence of discriminative pressure against the workers and unions.

'While the acquisition of new responsibilities by the unions implies a reinforcing of their power, security for their representatives, and facilities for their leaders to train themselves and acquire the necessary knowledge, in practice we can see the unions being fought, ignored or truncated every day, and faced with enormous difficulties in the execution of their rôle*'.

Despite all these obstacles, teams have come to the fore in a very short space of time, which promises well for the future, provided that a consistent effort is made to increase their numbers and improve their training in every sphere.

There are therefore two sides to the policy we must pursue. First the structural modification needed in a modern republic must be carried out with the greatest possible speed—relying initially on active personnel already equipped to do this, and who, from now on, can take on a good deal of the work involved. The second consists in training more and more able labour leaders as quickly as possible. The active participation of an increasing number of workers' representatives is simultaneously a guarantee of the independence and effectiveness of the unions, and a means of inspiring the working class as a whole with greater confidence in their future potentialities.

In strengthening a working class élite increasingly concerned with local and national responsibilities, we must never allow it to become detached from its roots. The bulk of the working class is interested primarily in action in factories, enterprises and industries, and the two kinds of activity must go hand in hand: one concerned with the state and general and regional planning, the other in industry itself, on the shop floor and in dealings with employers.

---

* Edmond Maire, Deputy Secretary General of the Chemical Industries branch of the CFTC (*Confédération Française des Travailleurs Chrétiens*), a large and mostly Catholic union, *L'Express*, 16 August 1962.

Trades Unions in Industrial Enterprises

A memorandum drawn up by the CFTC reads:

'A union's strength lies in its potential capacity for organising the industrial workers. . . . The most important aspect of union activity occurs within industry and business itself. It is there that the primary uses of the trades union movements can be seen most clearly, and there that the clashes which become national problems originate, it is there that conflicts and arguments begin. . . . It is surprising, therefore, to hear someone admit that the unions have something to do with the undertaking of a particular set of responsibilities, or with the elaboration of a particular policy (for example, the regional economic policy), when the same speaker denies the importance of union life at a lower level, or imagines that these problems do not exist in industry. . . . The representativeness of the whole organisation on a national level, or even of the branches concerned with a particular industry or trade, is largely determined by the effective weight carried by its individual unions, and the influence they exert over employees in industry'.

Already the unions are the official intermediaries in dealing with certain problems, social negotiations, wage conflicts, etc. In the event of a strike, even one not initiated by the union, no agreement can be reached without union help. The employers are under no illusions about this*.

This situation is a fairly recent one. The least spectacular, perhaps, of the reforms of the *Front populaire* in 1936, but constitutionally the most original, was the law which created collective conventions and so gave the unions a new legal function. Official negotiations between the employers and the unions have, in fact, developed only since then, and this fact

---

* In the words of Mark Serratrice, a French union official, the unions have become: 'in so far as they are the representative intermediaries, one element in the balance of industrial relations, even when these relations are in a state of tension'. *Stratégie patronale et Stratégie ouvrière vues à travers la Métallurgie*, in *Perspectives Socialistes*, August-September 1962.

is so striking that some people today regard it as the most characteristic and effective of all union functions. This is true even in the Civil Service, where, theoretically, the conditions of work do not depend on contract, but on a statute laid down by the State. In practice, the power of the unions has introduced a real contractual element into the solution of the problems which arise.

How can this kind of participation in business and social affairs be reconciled with the French unions' traditionally truculent attitude? Pierre Le Brun and André Barjonnet (who is the Communist Party's official Trades Union theoretician) have thrown a good deal of light on this in an article in the *Encyclopédie française*. They say:

'Disagreements, clashes and discussions are not mutually exclusive. They oppose and react on one another to form a continuous dialectical whole. There are few social conflicts, however violent, which do not ultimately end in discussion: in the traditional picture of trades union battles, strikes occupy the foreground. In history, however, negotiations play a fundamental part. But, however constant the discussion, complete agreement is rare. Usually there is a compromise. The temporary balance of power enshrined by compromises is often the source of future disagreement, and so conflict is born again out of the agreement itself. . . . (Finally) the discussions are as important as the disagreements'.

Coming from two active CGT officials, this statement is a fairly courageous one. Nevertheless, collective negotiations do have a truly revolutionary significance in that they establish the unions as a concrete, rival power to that of the management.

Since 1936 the worker has no longer had to face his employer alone in an argument in which he was fated always to get the worst. Instead, his cause has been taken up by the unions and the union delegates who speak in his name. A new balance is being struck.

Starting from this point the French trades union organisations are striving to develop and consolidate their position in

industry. Some aspects of modern industrial life help this
evolution. The higher qualifications demanded by industry, the
youth of large numbers of workers and technicians (a factor
which will be increasingly important in the future because of
the bulge in the population), the relative security resulting
from full employment (which has been kept up fairly well in
France in the last few years), the introduction of team work (in
contrast to the old system of one man to one job): all these
things encourage union membership inside the factory and
workshop. This situation is even more pronounced in the more
advanced sectors of industry (such as electronics, electrical
engineering, oil, chemicals, etc.) where trades unionism is
appreciably more widespread than in trades and professions of
the traditional type.

The evolution thus observed creates a direct link between
the claims of the workers and the conditions in a particular
industry. Even if this is composed of several different, widely
geographically separated establishments, union pressure tends
to be exerted in terms of the economic facts relating to the
industry as a whole, its financial potentialities and prospects
of expansion. More and more, attention is becoming concentrated, over and above the factory or workshop, on the
whole of an industry as a distinct, economic unit.

If conditions of work or pay depend strictly on a particular
firm's position, then the union must be fully informed about
exactly what this position is. If it is it will take a close interest
in the way it is run, both from a technological (time and motion
study, equipment, etc.) and an economic (soundness of investment, direction of production, etc.), point of view. These
points are recognised in some recent industrial agreements.

The report of the Jean-Moulin Club: *L'Etat et le Citoyen*,
mentions this trend as important. It points out that the more
aggressive of the workers' organisations distrusted industrial
agreements at first; they regarded them (sometimes justifiably)
as 'paternalist traps'. But lately major companies have been
able to negotiate agreements and undertakings concerned with

the firm's general conduct on a basis of a sort of equality. The unions—including the CGT—have co-operated, reluctantly but with a genuine desire not to stand in the way of a development which seems to follow from the new character of industrial relations. The idea seems gradually to be emerging in some working class circles that industrial agreements might usefully replace the old local or branch covenants.

There is no real contradiction here. Agreements reached in particular firms are not incompatible with broader covenants. Ultimately, the individual agreements might fit into the wider schemes.

Occasionally the unions have managed to insert a clause in such agreements guaranteeing them control over promises made by the employers. A number of these recent agreements have even provided, in the unions' favour, some kind of right of investigation into the general conduct of the business, with the possibility of seeing the basic accounts. In other cases the management has committed itself to consult the union on any important proposals to alter working conditions or methods of production. This new right to know and criticise what is going on in an industry is an important step forward for the unions and all its effects have yet to be seen.

To sum up, the new image of the trades unions in the most modern and advanced industries is marked by strong union participation, by the development of the union's branches or sections and by greater interest in management decisions. Furthermore, distrust of the traditional forms of political conflict and its complement, the belief in the value of powerfully organised union action, have also taken on a more modern appearance. As a result responsible and active union men are being increasingly led to a deeper study of economic affairs as they affect the industry for which they work or as they influence the general situation. As economics encroach more every day into the field of politics, so the rôle of the unions, which was originally limited to defend the rights of the workers, takes on an increasing political significance.

All these victories put in doubt what could once have been called the absolute monarchical rule of the employers. Their uncontrolled power has suffered a series of crushing blows, especially in matters of internal discipline and the organisation of labour. Legal jurisprudence may remain very conservative, but in practice matters tend to change and evolve because of people's everyday behaviour and the terms of the negotiated agreements. Strong resistance is certainly put up, mainly in the medium-sized firms; and, as we have already seen, a sort of counter-attack is being launched against the trades unionists. So far the problems created by the dismissal of responsible shop stewards have not been satisfactorily dealt with in France (except in the nationalised industries where more liberal provisions are often made). New protective measures involving appropriate procedures must therefore be brought into play whether within industry itself (disciplinary committees from employees and management, etc.), or outside it (court protection based on improved legislation). One reform which must come will enable discriminatory measures taken against a worker (unfair dismissal, discipline, etc.) to be legally quashed. In certain cases at present a judge may award light damages, but he can never have a decision, even an unfair or irregular one, revoked outright.

Today's most important claim, in the eyes of all French unions, concerns the official recognition of the union's branch (or section) inside the factory or business. The justification for this emerges from every page of my book. Here, too, the nationalised industries have generally taken the lead. Their policies should be extended to all but the smallest industrial concerns. The way to create a more natural balance of rights and duties, to ensure a more precise application of social legislation, and to encourage a feeling of confidence in the working class, is to recognise the consequences of union rights on an industrial level, and allow them to operate openly, by means of regular meetings between unions and employers, instead of by sporadic encounters in moments of crisis and conflict. To this should be added some procedure designed to settle the disputes about the exercise of union rights, whether individually or in concert, in order to obtain protection against unwarranted sackings, or unfair discrimination against active union leaders.

Finally, with the recognition of the union's official position should go a fresh start to the activities of the *Comités d'Entreprise**. These *Comités* have not worked as effectively as it was hoped they would. There are many firms where the committees have either disappeared or never even been set up. Where they do exist, they carry out only a fraction of their duties. The 1945 statute gave them control of all social welfare work within the firm. Usually they have been allowed to exercise this function and still do, in nearly every case. But in contrast, article three of the statute and the other provisions involving participation in managerial matters have remained a dead letter (again, the exception is a few of the nationalised undertakings).

To begin with, admittedly, the elected representatives of the employees had not the general, legal and financial knowledge to enable them to cope fully with their new responsibilities. All the same, there was room for hope that with the help of habit and experience a new kind of relationship might have grown up between the workers' representatives and the employers, and that, fifteen years after the experiment was begun, the committees would have been able to play their proper part. But the employers have not encouraged the growth of a reform which they regarded with suspicion, and their representatives have frequently taken advantage of the inexperience shown by workers' delegates.

A new start is needed for the *Comités* involving the training of workers for responsibility. Today there are opportunities which did not exist after the Liberation. In spite of all obstacles, the unions, as we have seen, have trained a certain number of men who, in their turn, are capable of teaching

* See p. 129, footnote.

others. Moreover, recent French legislation and a number of orders made by the Courts have now made it possible for the *Comités* to award compensation for lost pay to workers on educational leave.

However, the employers will still have to change their attitude and agree to co-operate on a new basis. Further legislation is needed to ensure also that the committees are consulted effectively on matters concerning the organisation and general conduct of the business, are kept informed of the extent and distribution of profits, and given quarterly reports on the progress of the firm and its individual factories, projects for industrial and commercial investment, new products and so on. When any important innovation likely to alter the firm's structure and employment prospects is under consideration, the committee should be aware of the reasons which have led to the management's decision.

There are some matters on which the committees' approval should be sought, since they interest the workers more than the employer himself. They include hours of work, public holidays and holidays, the training of apprentices, terms of engagements (in order to avoid discrimination on political grounds, and black-listing), technical training of workers, hygiene, safety devices and so on. It is here too that solutions can be sought to the problem of collective dismissals (criteria for determining the orders of priority in dismissals because of redundancy) and of the sacking of individuals, and so forth.

A better presented Plan and a clearer description of its aims by productive branches, as described in Chapter Seven*, would greatly facilitate mutual control. For the principal sectors of production, the Plan should incorporate monographs on the standard industry, describing the kind of development best adapted to the needs of the programme: the relative volumes of investment and turnover, etc. Descriptions of this kind would be designed to clarify the discussions of the *Comités*

---

* See pp. 128 and 129.

d'Enterprise and so lead to a greater awareness of the policy the firm ought to follow in order to achieve the Plan's aims. It is no easy matter for the union delegates to interpret in terms which are appropriate to the conditions of a particular firm the sort of purely economic directives they get in the French Plan at the present time.

If the sum total of these proposals were to be adopted, they would result in a profound modification of the social climate. The workers would no longer feel that they were being treated as passive elements, like tools or robots, but as human beings, able to face prosperity or hardship (the principal danger being that of unemployment*). The industrial committee would become a real forum for discussion, the exchange of information and opinions, and for constructive co-operation.

Trades Unionism and Democracy

Economic and technological changes mean that the labour organisations are faced with new responsibilities and many labour leaders are contemplating these with some understandable anxiety.

But what is taking place is a natural development. The acquisition of more rights and greater outlets for action involves facing up to wider and more difficult tasks. This is what maturity means, and it is a natural development in social life, just as it is in the life of the individual.

Today the unions are reaching maturity in the State as well as in the factories. They cannot turn their back on the problems this change brings about. There must be a common under-

---

* One of the large unions with Socialist principles, the CGT-FO (*Confédération Général du Travail—Force Ouvrière*) has stated in a pamphlet: 'We do not want to go on being strangers in industry, or mere cogs in a complicated machinery. In future, instead of feeling that the human element is treated on much the same level as machines or raw materials, we aim to understand the results of our labours, to see where it is going, to contribute of our own free will to a task of whose importance we are fully aware'.

standing of the difficulties involved and a common effort to find the solution to them.

The unions have long been the opponents of the State simply because the State itself was capitalistic and ultra-conservative. But as the State becomes more democratic—in social and economic as well as in political life—, as it guarantees more effective rights to the unions, so it ceases to be an adversary. A régime which is undeniably the instrument of economic prosperity and social justice is one which the workers will gradually come to be able to acknowledge as their own.

As they realise their growing importance, and the new conditions governing their actions the French unions are already beginning to recognise that they cannot ignore the political setting of their actions.

As Edmond Maire has put it*: 'The power of the unions cannot be exercised with equal effect in any type of régime; democratisation of industry and the whole economy require a new political climate. The usefulness of the unions requires political democracy, quite independently of economic democracy. From this point of view the reconstruction of political democracy in France is our major problem'.

The *Fédération des travaux publics et des Transports*, a branch of the CGT-FO, stated in April 1962 that 'the unions will bear a collective responsibility for the future of democracy'; and added: 'the reconstruction of democracy is the permanent task of the unions'.

This is the beginning of a development which may have considerable consequences in the future.

* *L'Express*, 16th August 1962.

CHAPTER NINE

REGIONAL
LIFE

THERE ARE a number of voices raised from time to time to protest against excessive centralisation in France. This criticism, which has become general, is well founded and indicates more than mere uneasiness. Centralisation is a crying need of the country, and any reorganisation of existing institutions in terms of the economic responsibilities of the State must take it into account.

The existence of the region as an economic fact has so far found no concrete institutions to stand for it, no mode of action, and no organisation endowed with the power of making decisions for it.

Nevertheless territorial development has become one of France's major problems. Within a very few years the natural growth of the population, the immigration of more French nationals from overseas and the free movement of labour envisaged by the Common Market will enlarge the population of France from forty-five to fifty-five million. This means the provision of more jobs. This has been done in West Germany. There balanced overall development and the even distribution of heavy urban concentrations over the country as a whole has ensured plentiful, varied employment and prosperous industrial activity, and has enabled millions of refugees to become productive members of the community. If left to itself, the economic situation in France might develop on very different lines.

151

France is suffering from an increasing demographic and economic imbalance. She has only one large, modern industrial city: the capital, and this houses one-fifth of the entire population and absorbs a considerable share of the country's available forces. On the other hand, more than half the country (Brittany, the Massif Central and the South-West) is turning its back on the highly developed side of Europe and is becoming more markedly backward all the time. Unless something is done about this, young people will find that new jobs are only available to them in limited geographical areas i.e. in the neighbourhood of Paris or one of the twenty or so other *départements* already associated with the mainstream of European development). Failing this they will have to go abroad to places where the process of development is increasing at a much faster rate than in France. As a result, the north-east corner of France will become absorbed into a Europe dominated by the Rhine, while the peripheral areas, deprived of their human and economic substance, will degenerate, with no exaggeration, into the 'desert of France'.

Even assuming the introduction of planning for Europe as a whole (the need for which has been demonstrated), and the solidarity of our partners (of which we cannot be absolutely sure), the development of the threatened areas will not follow automatically merely from investments realised with the help of the State or the community. Naturally, everything should be done to increase the volume of capital from outside to be put at the disposal of the less dynamic regions. Finally, however, their development can be achieved only by a voluntary, collective effort by the people concerned, within a structural framework which must be quickly established. External aid may to some extent supplement local initiative when this is inadequate or has lost heart, but it is not simply an excuse for those involved not to continue the task with their own means and on their own responsibility.

The Regional Economic Councils
How are the populations of backward areas to set about
achieving their revival and recovery?

First, it is necessary for each economic region in France to be
able to meet and compete on equal terms with the forces it will
encounter later. The *département* of Meurthe-et-Moselle cannot
hope to compete with the Ruhr. An area with much greater
material and financial resources, as well as man and brain
power, is needed for such a competition.

At present France is divided into twenty-one 'programme
regions'. It is generally agreed that this is too many and that
there must be some regrouping in order to create more
powerful units which could then be endowed with universities
and administrative offices adequate to their particular needs
and potentialities.

The region should be created around a capital, similar to the
ten biggest industrial cities which exist in the Common Market
and to which, except Paris, there is no exact equivalent in
France. Each of these regional capitals should constitute an
active and influential centre for industry, commerce, higher
education, administration and culture and be supported, if
necessary by subsidiary capitals. The division of activities
between the regional capital and its subsidiaries should be one
of the first subjects discussed by the regional authorities when
they are set up.

'If the geographical, social and professional groups which
go to make up the nation as a whole are to take a real part in
the elaboration of a Plan . . . then their counsels and decisions
must come in at all stages in the planning process and concern
every aspect of it.' If we agree with this proposition, put
forward by Bernard Gournay, and if we do not stop, as he
does, after considering the formulation of the Plan, but also
take its execution into account; if we mean discussion not only
'at all stages' but at all levels of the Plan's conception and
application—then it is clear that the region will be called upon
to play a decisive rôle. For on the human level it constitutes a

153

living fact where important communal matters can be dealt with and a solution reached of problems of whose existence the more responsible elements in the provinces are already fully aware. Professor Lavau had pointed out that the dimensions of the region make it the ideal setting for the new leaders who are emerging from trade and agricultural unions, universities and elsewhere. In this environment, faced with immediate objectives, they will be able to express themselves best and display positive qualities, without acquiring the bad habits to which politicians are liable.

If the 'regional revolution' is to work, then the region's representatives must play a direct part in economic policy and the application of the Plan. They will supply the main elements of the regional economic council, the basic instrument which will be to the region what the Economic and Social Council is to the nation as a whole. Its composition must be carefully studied if the mistakes and inadequacies of the present regional and departmental Development Committees are to be avoided. The goal ahead is, in fact, to make economic life completely democratic and to make sure that all interests, labour, commerce, agriculture, industry, the liberal professions and so on, are better represented. Apart from this socio-professional element, the regional council could also include delegates from the departmental General Council and representatives of important institutions such as universities, nationalised industries, major ports, etc. Accordingly, the composition of the regional economic councils will vary from one place to the next according to the local social and economic bias, with the object of creating as faithful a picture as possible of the activities of the area.

It would be as well, too, that the members should be able to devote a good deal of their time to their duties and have the necessary facilities at their disposal: this means that they would need financial compensation, especially when members are working men. Hitherto these men have been able to take only a limited, and sometimes purely nominal part in the work of the

154

Development Committees because they have not been compensated for loss of time or pay, or for travelling and accommodation expenses.

The rôle of the regional economic council can be effective only in so far as it is backed by an executive authority. There is no authority on a regional level at the present time other than the conferences which take place at long intervals and are attended by the Prefects and some Civil Servants.

In future the region should be permanently equipped for administrative action, which means that it must have someone at its head, a man of influence, perhaps someone of ministerial rank. This new administration would be in control of the regional budget, draw administrative credits (financed by contributions provided by the *départements*, in proportion to their contribution to the prosperity of the region) and credits for economic activities and measures corresponding to the region's part in the national Plan*.

The economic services as a whole (which are at present disseminated, some within a framework of various administrative subdivisions, and others on a basis of *départements*) will be regrouped in the regional capital. Economic services which are to be left in towns of less importance would in future be only subsidiary and dependent on the civil servant in charge in the regional capital.

The regional council will coordinate the activities of all regional, departmental or local economic organisations, both those in existence and those to be set up. Ideally it should combine and absorb a certain number of the existing ones and so put an end to the heaving mass of groups and sub-committees which are too often an additional factor in causing delays and complications. It has been calculated that in Lille alone there are one hundred and thirty-seven institutions and organisations at work on a regional level. This multiplication means a dilution of responsibility and a great waste of energy.

---

* See p. 156.

One of the first duties of the new regional economic councils is to take the place of some of these organisations and to define the spheres of activity of others more closely.

The regional councils and the economic administration which would go with them will submit their proposals to the government and to the national planning authorities for eventual incorporation in the national Plan. But their most important responsibility will still lie in the executive field. To this end it is desirable that in future the presentation of the national Plan should be modified in such a way that two kinds of business can be clearly distinguished:

First comes anything of incontrovertible national importance, (large basic investments, destined to benefit the nation as a whole or a major territorial part of it); matters of this sort will continue to be administered by the planning authorities and the ministries responsible.

Secondly, anything spread more or less evenly throughout the country with, in all cases, purely local effects. These affairs should be reorganised in the form of regional Plans, which would really be slices of the national Plan. Each of these regional Plans would have its own budget, to be allocated by the senior civil servant in charge of regional economy and by the regional economic council. The sums voted in this budget would enable them to carry out the national Plan in their own sectors, with a broad delegation of powers. They would distribute the credits allocated (housing, schools, public works, etc.) and the subsidies; decide the priorities involved, and coordinate industrial, agricultural and other investments, financed or subsidised by the State, in public or private concerns. They would be responsible for the development of proper educational establishments, universities and technical colleges, for training young people and providing additional instruction or refresher courses for adults after taking regional needs into account. They would decide the principles on which credit policy should be based (especially in the agricultural

156

field), lay down general rules for rural development*, and also determine the specific provisions needed in order to enforce the laws relating to land policies or problems concerning the marketing of agricultural products. As time goes on such laws will be applied with increasing consideration for the specific conditions in different regions. It is up to the regional councils to decide upon the best method of application in their jurisdiction and see that it is carried out.

Consequently it will no longer be necessary to refer to Paris about every individual decision, as is the case today. Apart from the overriding authority exercised by the senior civil servant in charge of regional planning—an authority which will be essential if the basic intentions of the Plan are to be observed faithfully—there will be maximum freedom and flexibility in the way the Plan is carried out within the region.

Decentralisation on this scale implies a large measure of self-government in the allocation of public money. The identical rules and regulations which today govern each individual decision taken in every region, borough or university will be abandoned†. An element of variation appears highly desirable in every sphere: specialisation of establishments for higher and technical education, housing, agricultural expansion, professional organisation, etc.

This regional council will establish a working relationship between the economic actions of the State and its organisations on the one hand, and the regional situation and the producers and consumers who will be carrying out the schemes and benefiting from them, on the other. This is an important aspect of democratic planning.

This can be further extended by an interpenetration between the regional councils and the national Economic and Social

---

* See below, p. 158 *et seq.*

† The official or officials responsible for taking a particular decision in Paris usually impose uniform regulations or, at best, take into account a limited number of possibilities. Solutions to fit particular cases can only be evolved at a regional level.

Council. Representatives of the regions (nominated by the regional economic councils) will be expected to take their places in the Economic and Social Council.

Finally, the setting up of regional economic councils and regional administrations will encourage trades union and professional organisations to build larger headquarters in the regional capitals, since this is where they will be most effective. It is in fact in the regional capitals that general conferences, negotiations concerning labour disputes and wage agreements etc., will take place.

Rural development schemes

A great many rural communities—especially the smaller ones—are unable to provide the social services which are as much the right of the country dweller as they are of the townsman. The only way of being sure that these can be installed economically is by concentrating the services and utilities concerned to some extent. A number of villages in every *département* should be designated as centres for the establishment of collective services. They should be chosen in order to be within easy reach of people in isolated communities. They would then supply these people with the social, economic and cultural facilities they very often lack in France today.

These include:

1 schools and vocational training centres (particularly in agricultural areas) catering for fairly large numbers, by means of the school bus services, and therefore in a position to employ highly qualified staff. *The provision of adequate teaching staff is an essential factor in revitalising and modernising rural areas.*

2 hospital facilities, and a maternity home, served by one or more doctors, a dentist etc., as well as providing consulting rooms for specialists paying regular visits.

3 one or more doctors, pharmacists, midwives, veterinarians, welfare workers, nurses etc.

4 an asylum small enough to be human.

5 sports and cultural facilities (stadium, swimming pool etc.).

6 local public services and some local administrative offices: postal and financial services, local government offices etc.

7 business services, such as the Agricultural Bank, friendly societies, cooperatives, the *Centre d'études techniques agricoles*, agricultural advisory boards etc.

8 recreational facilities such as a Community Centre, library, cinema etc.

The reorganisation of social and administrative life in the provinces will be the task of the regional authorities, working along general lines laid down in a new law. They will each have to prepare a development scheme, to be spread over a period of ten to fifteen years, which taken as a whole, will form an important part of the preparation of further Plans.

Little by little we shall see new methods of marketing and distribution centring in these key villages, with up-to-date craftsmen and good hotels and tourist amenities. All these are indispensable if centres of industrial development are to be created all over the country and if these are to be part of a coherent, overall plan.

In some instances the nationalised industries can set an example of decentralisation in accordance with the policy of redeveloping rural areas. But the most interesting experiments along these lines involve agriculture and businesses concerned with the production of food, all of which must be developed in productive areas. Slaughterhouses, canning factories, saw-mills, plants for supplying animal feeding stuffs and so on should be built on the site where the raw materials are produced, in preference to areas where the product is used. The concentration of industry in the main consumption areas is already too heavy.

The existence of a social and educational infrastructure can obviously do nothing but help in the installation of industrial

159

centres in rural areas; this is simply one more indication of how necessary they are.

One condition of a policy of modernising provincial towns and village centres in such a way as to halt the disintegration of rural life is the existence of an élite of determined young peasants to form the essential kernel of the whole movement, without which it could not function. These centres which are to be revitalised or created afresh cannot be mere administrative extensions of the central government; they must be taken over by people who actually live there and so have a stake in their development.

Revitalising regional and local life in this way is a prospect that goes completely against the tradition of centralisation which has prevailed in France over the past two centuries. Even in those left-wing circles which have been most in favour of territorial redevelopment, the need for extensive decentralisation has not always been properly understood. Yet democracy can make no progress in the conduct of the nation's economy, unless lively centres of ideas and activity are created which will have a direct influence on the people themselves.

'Local democracy is an irreplaceable element in the people's education*.' It is the means for the youth and the best elements in the country to take up the tasks which are properly theirs, effectively and in their own environment.

---

* *L'Etat et le Citoyen*, Jean-Moulin Club 1962.

CHAPTER TEN

THE PLACE OF
THE CITIZEN

MODERN SOCIETY, as we have seen, is becoming increasingly characterised by State intervention in economic affairs: an inevitable factor in a true democracy.

This development involves very strong tendencies towards centralisation and technocracy, which places greater power in the hands of technicians and officials. Whatever their type of government, the great nations of today have to face the dangers of bureaucracy and technocracy which may result in new forms of oppression for the individual citizen.

Unless the people of the western world want to find themselves living in the type of horrifying society described in some novels of the future; such as the hierarchic, calculating society of highly specialised dehumanised humans described by Huxley or the totalitarian one with its terrifying degree of mechanisation, they will have to radically reorganise their idea and practice of democracy.

The key to this reorganisation lies first and foremost with the individual. He must act where he will be most effective, where he can take the initiative and where his abilities will be most useful—not only, as I have said before, on a regional level, but, going still further in the direction of decentralisation, also in local communities, unions, and organisations and associations of all kinds. Wherever there is something to be done there must be people willing and eager to take part in any

F   161 number of ways, from protesting and making demands, via argument and inspection to actually controlling and making decisions. All these methods of influencing affairs are worth while if they are inspired by the desire to serve the community.

Democrats (and by democrats I mean what José Bidegain has described as men ready to sacrifice time and effort to the common good), must possess not only a devotion to the cause but also strong faith in the possibilities of our times and a deeply rooted optimism. If anyone bemoans the fact that such men are not particularly numerous these days, it may be because the events of recent years have undermined such faith and optimism. But without them a technological civilisation is only too likely to become an inhuman one.

The individual often feels weak and ignorant when beset by the crushing complexity of present day problems, and by forces which are both colossal and anonymous. He may be tempted to take the easy way out and turn his back on the difficulties, deny their existence or, which comes to the same thing, give way to the limited, summary kind of demagogy sometimes used to exploit his feeling of vertigo. This is often the case with people who feel that they are either professionally or socially underprivileged (such as many *Poujadistes**), or whose political ideals are over-simplified or out of step with the times (such as a number of army officers). Unable to adapt, they hurl themselves in blind revolt against the world they live in. In fact they will no more be able to prevent the inevitable course of future development than they have been able to prevent the process of decolonisation. But they can cause serious disturbances, painful clashes and even, in certain circumstances, create a real threat of civil war.

Other people—and these are far more numerous—choose to forget their problems. They are like the invalid who finds the least uncomfortable position in his bed and then stays there, without moving, for as long as possible, trying to forget

* Followers of a French right-wing fanatic named Poujade.

his pain and the operation he will probably have to face sooner or later. They give up and wait passively for a miracle to happen. These are the people who boast of the fact that they are 'not interested in politics'; they leave it to others, and in doing so become unconsciously and to some extent accessories, and later victims. Even their power to vote—when they use it at all—is merely another way of abdicating from their responsibilities.

In the words of the Jean-Moulin Club: 'the diseases of the modern State—conservatism and totalitarianism—come more from the apathy of the electorate than from the extent of technological and administrative development'. It must also be admitted that this apathy on the part of the electorate can be largely explained (and even excused) by a quarter of a century's painful political experience in France: the defeat and the occupation, with a government preaching collaboration; the impotence and betrayals of the Fourth Republic; the permanent invitation offered to the people by the Fifth to withdraw from political activity in favour of a single man who, moreover, pursues a policy compounded of equivocation and beatings about the bush. Can we be surprised that so many of our countrymen give up the attempt to understand or form an opinion, give up doing anything, give up altogether? The only way to restore their confidence in themselves and in their rôle is to appeal to them, to give them a say in the affairs of the nation and in the myriads of smaller matters which go to make up the sum total of everyday life, the life of every cell in the nation.

The problem of knowledge and education naturally occurs here too. As I have emphasised repeatedly throughout this book, political change is largely conditioned by education: school, general information, the training of adults and young people, of all those who will conceive and carry out the necessary reforms. All these are vital elements. But if we really mean to go beyond the stage of traditional democracy, of government by representation, to one of participation, then

163

appropriate methods must be brought into play. At this new stage, democracy will no longer be confined to ballot papers, motions for debate, or even to criticism; it will spread into numerous other activities, professional, cultural, trades union, as well as political. These activities must be on a human scale, in other words they must correspond to the facts of social life as everyone understands them; and they must give everyone a grasp of concrete facts, so that each individual can gauge the progress of his own personal efforts and of their success.

Democracy at the Grass Roots

There are two spheres of activity so important that I have devoted special chapters to them: they are regional decentralisation* and trades unionism†. But wherever there are communities of people, wherever there is a common need, wherever the public must be informed of the existence of a problem and must be able to participate officially, wherever collective decisions take place, the appetite for common effort must be allowed to reveal itself through organisations which work democratically.

Already we can see a kind of decentralisation on a vast scale beginning to take shape, going far beyond regional decentralisation, and not purely geographic. Some of the organisations I mention will be of limited duration and will disappear once they have served their purpose. Others fulfil a permanent need but their membership is more or less temporary (youth hostels, and parents' associations, for instance). Still others continue for an unlimited period; these range from municipal councils to cultural societies, and include cooperatives of every kind, tenants' associations, people's educational centres, and also, of course, professional groups, political parties, etc.

When people fail to combine in order to undertake something which is necessary for the common good, then the gap is either filled by the administration or by 'usurpers' who claim to act

---

* Cf. Chapter Nine. p. 151.
† Cf. Chapter Eight. p. 131.

in the name of those who have nothing to say for themselves.

The existence of clubs, cooperatives and representative groups, on the other hand, erects a barrier of 'compensatory powers' confronting the central authority, and is thus able to limit the encroachment of bureaucracy. While the Administration quite naturally tends to regard itself as an end in itself, these organisations are concerned with human aims and can replace impersonal rules and regulations with flexible and easily adaptable disciplines which everyone can understand and therefore accept.

Furthermore, in order to achieve their aims, all these essentially democratic groups can be brought to act in unison with other similar groups: unions of teachers can discuss matters with student organisations or with parents' associations, peasant cooperatives with trade unions or soup-kitchens and canteen managers etc. From these meetings a social intermingling, a better mutual understanding and a deep sense of solidarity should emerge and all will contribute to a truer civic spirit.

A large number of associations are already prepared to work in this way. Here there is a move towards self-government in a social centre, a youth hostel, or a tenants' association; there students are found taking part in the administration of the university, and in social and other affairs; elsewhere a block of flats forms a cooperative, a number of farmers make themselves collective owners of some farm machinery, people form a club and organise touring holidays as a party or reach for cultural wealth that would be beyond their individual means.

Schemes of this kind appear everywhere. It is as though the old society, made up of numbers of independent atoms, is gradually being replaced by a molecular society where the atoms cling together among themselves. The encyclical *Mater et Magistra* defines it in these terms: '. . . socialisation is one of the characteristic aspects of our age . . . . The tendency is to associate with a view to attaining goals which are beyond the means and capacities of the individual.'

France today is supposed to be apathetic and non-political,

and yet this process of association is increasing, especially where new forces are awaking and coming to grips with acute problems (as is the case in rural areas). Many more of them could exist, among the young in particular, given the right help.

But from now on a whole parallel representative system is beginning to be established*. As soon as it is recognised and consolidated by the State it will form a new democracy, becoming close-knit and generalised, and releasing huge

---

* M. Joseph Rovan made a perceptive study of this rapidly expanding phenomenon in his book *Une idée neuve: la Démocratie*, particularly in the following passage: 'Men and women who want to be useful or to bear some responsibility and authority . . . have begun to express themselves in working on behalf of a particular milieu, a profession or part of a profession, a district, a locality, in the name, in fact of any more or less stable group which finds itself in a common situation, and in a situation which calls for changes to be made. . . . A whole parallel representative system is beginning to establish itself in France, alongside the traditional political system, but having an effect on this through research and study groups which are growing up spontaneously nearly all over the country, especially since the spring of 1958. These new public figures are emerging in the unions and among the representatives of industrial workers by regrouping and new, unorthodox means of action; in family associations and groups, in leisure and holiday associations; in the professions; in the wheels of State which already, although it often goes against the grain, allow for some consultation and participation by groups and individuals concerned in a particular sphere of development; and in communal or para-communal life. They appear, in short, wherever the majority of citizens, either formally or by implication, succeed in having a say in the elaboration of decisions which concern their own lives, through official channels, and also, very often, spontaneously and unofficially. . . . The new leaders of opinion . . . enjoy a considerable margin of confidence from their fellow citizens and exercise a considerable influence over them. They have greater knowledge and experience (especially after they have been carrying out their tasks for some time), they come into contact with other spheres of life, they possess a certain (often innate) gift for expressing succinctly the feelings, needs and opinions current in the sphere they represent. They receive and transmit information from within this sector to the outside world and from the outside world to their own sector. Their function is simultaneously to represent and to express, to interpret and transmit, to act and to inspire'.

166

quantities of energy which today are either lost or ignored.

If the central power is truly republican and anxious not to lose contact with the nation, and to interpret its wishes and feelings, it will find opportunities in this hive of activity for the exchange of information, support against selfish or too narrow interests, and also against the routine of its own administration. It will see in it a sign that civic life is on the move. Its dearest object will be to help democracy sweep through the country like electricity through a circuit, making it shake and shiver into action. Far from distrusting such good intentions a central authority should encourage them, and where necessary, provide them with material facilities, such as premises, tax relief etc., and above all else show them the understanding which old-fashioned administrations are generally quick to deny to private initiative.

In the same spirit, local associations should be given greater freedom and independence through a loosening of the supervision which now often blunts all sense of responsibility.

The Political Parties

There is one form of association that falls within the framework of this summary of free activities which I have not yet discussed, and which would nevertheless appear to be the model for all voluntary, self-determining associations. I mean the political party.

It is legitimate, respectable and even necessary for the implementations of programmes and ideologies, that men sharing the same convictions should band together in order to spread or defend their common beliefs. But it is because in France in the past these parties have often forgotten their programmes and ideologies—or have sacrificed them to more immediate ends—that they are devalued, or even discredited today. This is what men mean when they speak of the party crisis.

There are some who think that the same methods of action and propaganda which were devised for an epoch when pure politics alone occupied the front of the stage, are no longer suitable for a time when the struggle is basically one for control of economic facts. It is, indeed, perfectly true that French parties have not made the necessary efforts to adapt, and that their workings and methods have changed very little. This gives the impression that they are existing in an abstract situation which has nothing to do with reality, that they persist in flogging dead horses in words which are scarcely less so, at one moment, and waiting for a brave new world which is always being postponed indefinitely, at the next. The active party member devotes his evenings to discussions which he must often know to be pointless, and to proposing motions which will never be followed up; he wears himself out selling papers, posting bills, canvassing from door to door for a public which grows daily more indifferent, and attending demonstrations with no future to them. He never sees the results of his efforts, and occasionally his sacrifices. This is as true of the party member in Paris, who lives and acts in close proximity to his chief political leaders as it is of his equivalent in a small provincial town. Meanwhile the democratic activity of the country is passing into the hands of other groups who, in contrast, are working on a basis of concrete facts and trying to solve problems which have a direct bearing on the present and near future. So true is all this, that cooperatives and rural action societies have grown up outside the party framework* and have sometimes encountered hostile reactions, not only from the extreme conservative elements, but also from left wing parties and organisations.

And yet, when political parties disappear—either because they have fallen into disuse or have been suppressed by authority and compelled to give way to one single party (which, because there is only the one, will not be a political party at all, but something else, then democracy will disappear with them. It is not a matter of chance that in France they have

---

* This is not the case in other countries, for example in Belgium or Switzerland.

been guilty of errors, or that today they are marking time or in retreat: their fate coincides with a weakening of democracy itself. But it does not necessarily mean the inevitable decline of either one thing or the other.

There are, certainly, some political parties which ultimately fade away. But when they all seem to have been hit it indicates, rather, that in their own way they are reflecting a real climate of opinion. At a time when the forces of democracy as a whole are in retreat, when the tempo of political life is slowing down, when too many people are tending to fall back on their private concerns rather than face the great and difficult problems of the day, then the political parties will also become sleepy.

What we have to hope is that they will put this time to good use in order to examine their own consciences and reap the necessary educational advantages from their experiences. If they have been weak in the past it is because they have not remained unyieldingly faithful to their vocation and their commitments, and it is for this, more than anything else, that they are to blame. They must avoid falling back into this error against democracy by coming back to democracy. And first of all this must be so in their internal organisation: the party should not be the tool or plaything of a little nucleus of expert politicians (called the machinery), but the organisation through which a whole sector of public opinion can express its desires and aspirations. It can only fill this rôle properly if the active members who are its foundations insist on being heard again in council. This is the way to reform and revive the political parties in France.

On the other hand, parties can recover their influence only to the extent to which their members are involved in all the concrete activities I have discussed above. Everyone taking an active part in politics should also be an active member of a union, cultural circle, cooperative or some similar association. In this way his party's political views will stand a chance of being based on facts, developed from real experience, and from

F*   169 problems and aspects of real life*. Once this happens the parties will be able to bring their doctrines to maturity and draw up their proposals in terms which the public can begin to understand again.

Such of the parties which will manage to accomplish this reconversion will find, in addition, an echo which they have lost. Whether we like it or not, political parties cannot vanish in a free country. They are there to meet a genuine need, and that need will not cease to exist because the parties have failed in their duties in the past. With no political parties alongside them, other positive and practical activities are in danger of developing within too narrow a field and so becoming too specialised. Economic organisations are groups with a natural tendency to limit themselves to day-to-day, empirical and occasionally selfish action. In cultural organisations, the total freedom of argument which is, in fact, highly necessary, promotes a random harvest of ideas which are often confused and to some extent irresponsible.

Political foresight, however, which is an essential quality of a party, makes it possible, on the one hand to take the long view of specialised activities, and encourages thinking beyond the immediate experience to consider the whole; while, on the other, it enforces a choice of priorities in aims and means, and the subordination of each particular decision to a general orientation which has been arrived at in common.

The Peasant Example

The ideas set down in the beginning of this chapter are nowhere more thoroughly applicable than in the agricultural field. The problem here is to find an effective way of reconciling the social and human factors, which cannot be ignored, with the demands of a rapid technical evolution which is as yet far from complete. This reconciliation can only come about

---

* Industrial and agricultural unions already do this, and this is why they exercise a much greater influence over their members than the parties do today.

through the awareness of the bulk of the peasant population itself, and by the action these people take.

Out-of-date agricultural conditions have now made it impossible for producers to compete with the organised interests which are growing up around them. The last century has seen enormous strides in the industries which supply the farmer's needs or process what he produces, as well as in marketing and finance, while the peasant has remained in more or less the same condition. Moreover there are a good many tasks and expenses today which can only be undertaken through the medium of properly constituted organisations.

The variety of the problems adds to an already complicated situation. Recent statements of Mr Pisani* insist rightly on the diversity and sometimes even contradiction between these problems as they appear in one region or another and between one product and another. Therefore, there can be no general rule or solution. We must be prepared for extensive decentralisation of authority and policy if the people in charge, put there by the interested parties themselves, are to be able to choose—within the general framework of the national and regional Plans—the methods which are best suited to their needs.

To all intents and purposes, the work of the French Cereals Office would have been impossible ever since 1936, without the technical and administrative participation of producers' cooperatives. If they had not existed beforehand, and if others had not been formed since, the Office would have been a heavily bureaucratic administrative institution and, taking into account the peasant mentality, it is fairly sure that it would rapidly have fallen apart. The real responsibilities given to the cooperatives put the major part of the machinery into the hands of the producers themselves, and as a result the Office has been immensely useful.

Over the past few years any number of interesting new ventures have sprung up at the level of the village or canton.

---

* French Minister for Agriculture.

The young farmers in such communities get together in a
CUMA* for the purchase of one or more machines which no
individual needs for more than a few days or weeks in a year
but which they can only safely afford between them. One
person within the group is made responsible for the whole
of a particular job (for example the milking), and is paid on a
basis of the hours' work he gives to the community. Meanwhile,
another member of the team will be responsible for marketing
a particular type of produce: milk, fruit, calves sold for veal,
and so on. This kind of venture will gradually spread, and
we may even see collective herds. There are numerous
examples of this kind of group because they tend to multiply
rapidly.

The development of 'group farming' is likely to encourage
the setting up of viable production units, and so introduce
fundamental alterations into the lives and working conditions
of farmers. It will be necessary to promulgate a law concerning
the different forms these cooperatives should take and the
Agricultural Bank (*Crédit Agricole*) should also encourage
cooperation of this kind: in some cases it ought to refuse
assistance to individual farmers for particular types of investment when the tasks would be better undertaken in common,
and keep its resources for cooperative groups—or at least give
the latter priority.

Agricultural groups should not confine their activities to
production. They should carry them further. It is fairly clear
that the present state of affairs will not improve noticeably if a
group looks no further than one link in the chain of agricultural activity: they must also take an interest in production
and distribution.

The group could therefore undertake, for the benefit of all
its members, to make purchases and investments and strive to
add to the general store of knowledge and information, as well
as organising ways of preserving, conditioning and preparing

---

* *Coopérative pour l'utilisation du matériel agricole.* More than 10,000
agricultural co-operatives were in existence in France in 1962.

their produce and selling it in either home or foreign markets*. By taking charge of a growing part of the commerce and industry connected with food and agriculture, the group would reduce the number of middlemen and guarantee its members the profit which they never see at present. The main reason for the prosperity of Dutch or Danish farmers is because they are not restricted to their primary activities. By means of collective organisations they have become industrialists and businessmen, acting with a remarkable spirit of up-to-dateness and efficiency.

In sectors where organisations looser than cooperatives are needed, producers should nevertheless unite with a view to making joint contracts with collectors, processing firms and distributors.

In this way it will be possible to achieve a concentration of supply in response to a demand which is already highly concentrated. This happens when the produce is absorbed by a small number of manufacturers, or when the market is the monopoly of a few commercial chains. It is always a difficult and unequal process to reach agreement in a situation which demands that the producers should act in concert†. This is a similar step forward to that achieved by the French working class in 1936 when the principle of general labour agreements was laid down by law.

---

* There are several different kinds of cooperatives:

(*a*) Cooperatives for purposes of supply, which provide their members with the materials they need to purchase.

(*b*) Cooperatives for the purpose of providing facilities and services, which purchase for common use equipment, machines, breed-animals, etc., and also arrange the mutual exchange of working hours, etc.

(*c*) Cooperatives for processing, preserving and marketing agricultural produce.

† There are a million and a half producers of milk in France, while motor cars are turned out by only a few firms. Yet these two activities represent a roughly equivalent proportion of the national income. The milk producers will not be able to look after their own interests as effectively as the motor car manufacturers unless they combine on a local as well as a national level.

173

Unfortunately this tendency towards communal activity is continually coming up against pockets of resistance which, however small, have often proved capable of preventing the success of exceedingly interesting ventures. For this reason the most energetic agriculturalists in a number of cases are pressing for the recognition of the rights of cooperatives and unions when these represent a fixed proportion of producers and output over a given area. Groups whose representative character is beyond question should be allowed to lay down rules about organisation and discipline, with an eye to regulating the market, conditions of sale, quality of the product etc. The French Government has recently been empowered to extend such rules by decree to cover all farmers in a given area dealing with a given type of produce. This measure could be carried out in a number of ways: interested parties could be consulted by means of a referendum, or the demands of a qualified majority might be accepted, and so on. The main thing is that an effort towards self-discipline by a large majority should not be wrecked by a small, intractable minority who do not see where their stubbornness is leading.

Obviously the administration is not in a position to undertake the organisation of all agricultural life, only a few aspects of which have been dealt with here. If it were to do so the ensuing bureaucratic control would inevitably lead to rigid generalisations just where suppleness and adaptability were needed. Only active members of the agricultural population themselves, selected by their fellows to supervise their common interests, can manage simultaneously to create a freely acceptable discipline and a continuous adaptation to the technical needs of the time, provided that the requirements of the Plan are respected.

This is particularly true of the land development corporations (known as SAFER) which have recently been set up by law, but which are still a long way from finding their proper forms and laws. The object is to modify the conditions of agricultural life with a view to creating the maximum number of viable farms. Taking into consideration the variations in the soil and in the mental attitude of the people in different country districts, it is clear that SAFER's cannot do the good work that is expected of them unless they are run by men who are themselves members of the peasant population and therefore in a real position to understand and express peasant interests.

A growing proportion of the peasant population, especially among the young, the middle sized farmers, and those starting up in specialised fields, such as breeding or dairy farming, are beginning to realise that these conditions are necessary if development plans are to be a success. On all sides there are signs of collective activity and of organisations being born and developed on a highly democratic basis, and one which is well adapted to meet modern conditions.

Young people in the country are working together, carrying out investigations in common, finding out that they need unity: they are already acting upon their discovery. They are confronted with organised vested interests, outmoded structures and still powerful social forces, industrial organisations which are financially very strong, traditional or new chains of middlemen and so on. As a result their efforts lead them into still more widespread observations and they begin to be aware of politics—in the highest sense. By sharing their reflections on the problems and experiences of every day, by a series of fumbling advances, and an apprenticeship in working for the common good, they are discovering, together, the way towards the real solutions.

The New Civic Spirit

Lastly, we must look even further ahead—to the nation's fundamental needs. A country's political and economic institutions cannot make a democracy by themselves: they are no more than a framework for it. Neither are all the organisations I have been talking about, even if they must become more or less institutional, a democracy. The most deeply and sincerely democratic government can (and should) acknowledge,

175

encourage and support them, but it cannot create them out of nothing, or compel them to work; in any case that would be the reverse of democracy.

The truth is that there is no democracy without democrats at work. Democracy is first and foremost a state of mind, and it has to be voluntary or nothing.

What makes up this attitude of mind? The answer is, primarily a deep concern with the future of the community to which one belongs and a desire to take part in it at every level of understanding, decision and action; secondly, it is the feeling that no human life is complete if it is limited to the horizon of a single individual; it is the conviction, also, that this is not the best of all possible worlds, that reason and justice should hold a greater sway than they do and that their triumph is worth fighting for. This is the civic spirit which Montesquieu called virtue, or love of the Republic, which means literally of the thing that belongs to everyone.

But an individual citizen who is determined not to remain wrapped up in his private life must be ready to accept a certain amount of discipline: he must become the secretary of a group, or at least a steady member of it, he must give up time and effort to work which may sometimes be hard or unrewarding, and he must sacrifice his leisure and sometimes his sleep.

A working day is no longer the same as it was in the nineteenth century: it leaves time for the practice of more generalised democracy. It is up to the citizens to use part of the time they have gained to prepare for a future in which men will have still more free time and yet more opportunities in the world.

The experience of working as one of a group, of holding responsibility, of influencing others by one's actions, of the success of a common undertaking and of winning a victory over adverse circumstances: all these things constitute ways in which the individual can express himself. It gives to people who undertake the work the satisfaction of knowing that they have been useful to the community.

This civic spirit is emerging particularly among the younger generation in France. It is quite true that years of successive disappointments and lost illusions have made many young people turn away from abstract ideologies and theoretical arguments in favour of a more realistic standpoint dealing in facts and concrete evidence. But they do not have less civic spirit than their elders, they simply want to exercise it on direct achievements and precise objectives. They reserve their enthusiasms for problems of development, supply and organisation in their own region, job or profession, and will attend a CUMA* or union meeting more willingly than they will support the local branch of a political party. We must not only recognise these new human factors and allow them to emerge and grow, we must also adapt local and national institutions to fit them.

There is no doubt that this widely extended exercise of democracy is a way of combating the curious apathy which occasionally descends on some modern societies, epitomised at one moment by the teen-aged gangs and at another, by apparently crushing the crowds who fill the streets at the weekends. It is the boredom of an eternal present, closed in on itself and with nothing to look forward to.

An active and responsible person is in no danger of being bored even when he is engaged on a boring task. He avoids the curse of being passive and inert. He becomes one of those people who are 'more free because they are more committed†'; and he is filled with the spirit of the uplifting struggle in which he is taking part in order to achieve a future based on his own efforts.

In the last resort, this is what it is all about: the citizen is a man who does not leave it to others to decide his fate or that of the community as a whole.

Because democracy depends fundamentally on the will of the citizens, because it implies a constant effort, it can never

* See p. 172.

† Declaration of the *Centre national des Jeunes Patrons*, Deauville, June 1962.

come about by itself. One cannot go to sleep and expect democracy. It is a task requiring unremitting effort.

Just as it cannot come about by itself, so it can never be perfect. There is no such thing as a democracy that has been successfully achieved once and for all. It is a goal for the future, something which is always just over the horizon.

But because it can never be fully achieved, democracy is always being threatened. It is threatened by its opponents, naturally, but much more seriously by the carelessness or apathy of the citizens themselves. Only they can keep it alive, by carrying it along from day to day, in a constant communal movement towards progress.

CONCLUSION

CONCLUSION

THIS BOOK devoted to France's present day problems must be taken as a whole. If the proposals it contains have an economic as well as a political bearing, this is because the two subjects can no longer be separated. It would be a waste of time to look for solutions to our problems in a purely legalistic readjustment of our form of government. We must go further than that.

What we have to do now is to lay the foundations of a free, workable political régime; of more stable and energetic economic expansion, and of a social environment where the young will find new certainties.

Laying foundations is unrewarding work, and not particularly spectacular or uplifting. There is a temptation to try to build the first two or three storeys of the house before the foundations are properly in place. We must keep explaining to those who are, understandably, impatient, that the first essential is to ensure a stable base for the work to come, a finished foundation which can guarantee the success of the steps which come after it. Yes, first complete the foundation.

The general plan outlined in this book cannot be adopted piecemeal, because every part of it makes an essential contribution to the rest. There would be no point in taking up one sensible ingredient, and then allowing it to be warped and neutralised by the overall picture. There is no point in trying to prop up a system by purely legalistic methods when the

181

general policy does not interpret the people's wishes and so causes a wider and wider split between the people and those who govern them. There can be no point in giving the Economic Council broader powers, or consulting the unions more often, and at the same time fostering a growing distrust of the discipline required of the working classes and leaving the economy at the mercy of haphazard and improvised ventures, which (whether public or private) lack any unity or co-ordination.

France has suffered too often from this kind of shortsightedness in viewing things as a whole. Twice, in 1936 and in 1944, a terrific wave of public enthusiasm was allowed to die away bit by bit for want of a coherent overall plan, especially in the financial and economic fields. Unless a precise programme of economic action has been prepared in advance, no great political movement can ever make the most of a favourable situation and set the nation irrevocably on the path towards a new and better future.

There are people who imagine these changes will happen on their own, as part of the normal process of growth and maturity. All we have to do is wait patiently for them to come about. But there are still too many hazards, too much could still go wrong to allow us to relax our vigilance for a single instant.

Every day those who work and produce are becoming more aware of this. They may sometimes seem deeply suspicious of anything they call 'politics', but my travels through France have convinced me that in fact they have an eager curiosity to see the emergence of a plan to reorganise our institutions, so that we can face the future boldly, in readiness for other, more sweeping reforms.

This book is too long, but still it has not finished dealing with this subject. Because I have tried to confine myself to foundations and to fundamentals, I have had to leave out many other vital matters.

It is evident, for instance, that so long as knowledge and culture remain a minority privilege and so long as the public is fed on partial or tendentious information, doled out by the authorities or by interested parties—democracy will be either false or non-existent.

It is perfectly right and proper for a man to receive some kind of reward for his merits, but it goes utterly against the grain, and is not in the public interest, for his sons and his son's sons to assume and keep privileges which are denied to other children of their generation. The principle that privilege cannot be inherited is the only real answer to the class problem. Some kind of élite will develop in any society and this is inevitable and even desirable. But it must be constantly stirred up to see that it renews itself and does not become a caste. In no régime is this an easy matter: even Khrushchev in a recent speech deplored the fact that between sixty and seventy per cent of university and senior school students in the Soviet Union are the children of intellectuals and civil servants.

The key to human emancipation lies in giving all children equal opportunities through equality of education. One may fairly say that the masses will never feel that a decisive step has been taken in the direction of practical socialism until this reform has been fully implemented.

As for the problem of keeping the public informed—which arises each time in French history that the Republic and civil liberties have to be reconsidered, and which is magnified today in proportion to the scope of modern technical developments—this is, in the last resort, the king pin of a democratically planned economy. Time and again in the preceding pages, I have emphasised that a good many of the proposed reforms would not bear fruit unless in future the French people are kept precisely informed of the state of their economic affairs, of the difficulties that are being met and of the measures which might resolve them.

Political and economic progress thus implies reforming the general condition of public knowledge, and raising the level of adult education and information as well as that of young people.

Against these changes there are not merely undeniable practical difficulties, but also determined vested interests. That is why such changes will never see the light of day unless the nation gets a régime specifically adapted to deal with the problems of our time.

Indeed, no such régime is going to emerge by a lucky accident, a fortunate ballot or a well-meaning government. Far-reaching efforts are needed and success depends on the active participation of the country as a whole, and especially of those forces in it which, in conjunction, have always stood for progress. In the past whenever these elements—the underprivileged part of the country, which is always aggressive, or even revolutionary, the up-to-date and enlightened minority of the classes already in power, and the young people who instinctively look towards the future as their own—have united to strive for a single goal, vast changes have become possible and apparently insuperable problems have been resolved. The simple reason for this is that this section of the community holds the nation's reserves of energy and willpower.

While these elements remain passive, apathy and despondency spread and a great silence falls over the land; the unequal distribution of wealth goes from bad to worse, and the most obvious injustices seem to be tolerated, or at least regarded as inevitable by everyone. At the same time respect for the fundamental rights of man is imperilled.

For if there is one thing which presents a harsh picture of the fragility of political progress, it is the protection of the individual and his liberties against authority. Everyone, or nearly everyone agrees in principle. But reality, during the last few years, has given the lie in the most appalling way to the principles France has clung to for two hundred years. The most flagrant breaches of the law have occurred without the government's making any attempt to stop them; on the contrary, highly placed civil and military authorities have encouraged and even ordered them. The law has shown itself powerless to impede the increasing use of torture, arbitrary imprisonment, and the seizure of newspapers. Experience shows that the courts will act when the State injures private property: they have never behaved to the same degree as guardians of the people's liberties and the rights of man. They leave themselves open to the suspicion of class favouritism in the dispensation of justice.

There are no institutions so perfect that they are immune from accidents, and of course weaknesses will always appear. But the country will not be purged as its dignity demands until every abuse is denounced as soon as it appears. The authorities should not be complaisant, the press blasé or the law courts indifferent. New legal and administrative machinery (though these are indispensable) are not enough. They will work only if the pressure of awakened public opinion insists that unacceptable practices shall cease. Abuses will cease to be practised or tolerated in the name of justice and authority only when the citizens themselves make an outcry and proclaim their horror, disgust, and indignation. The behaviour of politicians, and that of judges too, depends in the last resort on the workings of democracy and strict adherence to principles which, in both the Fourth and Fifth Republics, has been lacking in Parliament, the political parties, the press and public opinion as a whole.

The renewal of contact between the army and the nation depends on a similar awakening. For years the French army has lived and fought a long way off; and the views it has adopted on many matters have been very different from those of the country as a whole. There has been very little contact between the French people as a whole and the army (which has, in any case, always been recruited from a very restricted social group). As soon as the army ceased to respect the State, its commands and its representatives because it no longer found them worthy of its ideals, the segregation had dramatic consequences. Governmental shilly-shallying, a number of im-practical pledges (which were never properly fulfilled because they were impractical), and the devious and disingenuous policy pursued in Algeria, all helped to undermine the army's trust in the civil authorities, and to break its habit of un-questioning obedience. In this way the army drew further and further away from the nation until it was eventually in oppo-sition to it.

While the armed forces became increasingly cut off from public opinion, there were many officers who came to the con-clusion that it was the virtues of the army which led to its being misunderstood; they felt that they were the one virile force in the land and sooner or later their mission to defend the glories of an ungrateful nation would be fulfilled*. The idea of the *pronunciamento* emerged. Those who thought about it appear to have had no qualms in taking for their models the under-developed countries where technical developments are so few and the social structures so weak that the army is very often the only force with any capacity for organisation.

There is only one possible defence against the risks involved, and that is to fight everything which tends to cut off the army from the nation†. It must be made to see that it is not an isolated political body, it must be made more aware of the needs and wishes of the people of which it is part and from which it must not become divorced, it must be made to share the hopes

---

* An answer received during the course of an inquiry carried out among officer cadets gives an apt illustration of this attitude: 'The army should not bow to the example of the Nation, but should lead the Nation to model itself on the army which is the only force capable of truly upright and selfless conduct'.

† To take only one example: it is not right that two types of youth should be brought up from their schooldays to be ignorant and suspicious of one another; it is the more wrong in that the soldier in the twentieth century is becoming ever more of a technician. The first reform is to incorporate the military colleges into the French University system, so that the officers, engineers and civil servants of the future may learn together that they must all perform a part in the same national task.

and preoccupations of the nation at large. Only the country itself can do this. But first it must make it quite clear that it will never yield to threats.

On 13 May 1958, the French army realised that the nation was turning away from its institutions. There were many officers who had no hesitation in expressing, even illegally, a feeling of disaffection, which they felt was general, against the régime. If in future Frenchmen sit back in silence and say nothing, the same officers might well feel that they had been deceived and made fools of and allow themselves to be carried away once more. This danger will persist until they realise that they would eventually come up against stiff resistance. If they feel perfectly certain of this, many of them would be reluctant to provoke a bloody battle between the army and the people, and to use against the nation the weapons and the young men she herself had entrusted to them.

Finally, the conduct of the ranks is affected by popular feeling and behaviour, and these react directly on the mentality and attitude of the officers.

Thus whether the blackmail which has been practised on the country in such a way as to leave a mark on its whole political life which will take years to erase, is to end or to reappear, depends to a great extent on the country itself.

In the absence of a clear, national will, separate bodies grow up here and there, minorities organise themselves and have a bad effect on the whole country—the more so in that they possess weapons. But when democracy defends itself, then the fragmentary, centrifugal forces which encourage disorderly conduct decrease at once.

It is up to all responsible men, political and trades union leaders, elected representatives and active people generally, to lead France towards the knowledge and practice of democracy. They must be untiring in their efforts to show the nation precisely where the problems lie and the various possible solutions, even if this needs courage, and even in the midst of the supposed trend away from politics which some people welcome joyfully.

Far from minimising the obstacles to be surmounted, they should call upon the nation to face up to them and prepare it to share actively in the work.

Waldeck-Rousseau, Clemenceau, Poincaré and Léon Blum shared this conception of their rôle: they believed it was their duty to mobilise the profoundest feelings of the nation and not, as has so often been done since, to shuffle or anaesthetise them. When they spoke to the people or their representatives it was not to produce vague generalisations, but to present them with definite proposals and policies and ask for decisions on them.

Each time, the country responded. Each time, it exercised its powers of arbitration and gave the government a mandate to overcome the opposition of parties, the political opposition and pressure groups.

When the country has an honest appraisal of the facts before it, even when these are apparently highly technical, even when they demand painful sacrifices, it does respond. The true statesman trusts the people. Then the people know that important decisions are really in their hands and they can rise to the situation.

When all is said and done, democracy can only live if the citizens and the leaders of the country behave as democrats. Churchill never had to resort to a presidential régime, or put pressure on Parliament, in order to be an inspiring political figure, because his frankness and courage in whatever he said and did, kept him in close touch with his countrymen; and because he never ceased to be a democratic leader of a democratic people. The licence given him by Parliament and people to carry out his task was based on a straightforward policy formulated on clearly and precisely stated principles, and never on a blank cheque. The objectives had been chosen by the nation, and it was the nation which chose the man to carry them out.

It is naturally easier to found and maintain an association of this kind at a time of great national emergency. It would be too pessimistic to assume that a great nation is incapable of sighting its targets and fighting to attain them, in time of peace.

Those who deny this are those who are afraid that by using democracy in this way, France will be steered in a direction which does not suit them personally. It is easy for anyone to see in what direction the country will develop in future if the forces of movement and progress are able to exercise sovereign influence, and if the power and initiative is put into the hands of the underprivileged sections of the community, of the young, and of all those elements most likely to find answers to its problems. If the framework within which we live at present is replaced by a real political and economic democracy such as the one I have tried to describe then clearly the country will go ahead with reforms in order to free itself from want, ignorance and injustice.

France today stands on a political threshold. The timid fear to cross this threshold. But among both peasants and workers, among students and their teachers, there is an increasingly pronounced feeling of impatience to cross—and it is this which will prevail in the end.

Talking to an audience of young men, in 1959, I assured them that the next fifteen years would be decisive, that they could bring disasters whose consequences would be felt for a very long time—but that they could also mark a turning point in our history that would offer a wealth of magnificent possibilities. Nearly four years have gone by since then. Is there anyone who would dare to say that they have been well spent in France?

The remaining ten years is the length of time which Khrushchev has estimated it will take his country to catch up with the production level in the United States, today the highest in the world. More and more, then, it is on grounds of the economic progress and achievement within their grasp that civilisation and ideologies will be competing.

In the realm of science and technology, ten years is a period which can bring about fantastic transformations, from the use of atomic energy in industry and production to the conquest of the sky.

189

Ten years is a space of time in which a new generation will grow to responsibility—not only in the political field but wherever there are decisions to be taken, whether these are economic, cultural, military or anything else. It will be a generation unmarked by the miseries and humiliations of the last few decades, but knowing enough about them, approaching their task with eyes wide open, with clear ends in view and sufficient impetus to overcome the obstacles in their way.

Moreover ten years is time for the under-developed parts of the world to achieve political independence and move forward along the road to economic independence as well. In less than ten years the under-developed countries will have fixed certain basic formulae—empirically, as the young always do—which may perhaps give a new character to a whole epoch.

With prospects of this kind closing around them all the time, the French people can no longer afford to let themselves drift.

Now is the time for a clearsighted and determined choice.

One or two generations have allowed their chances to be ruined. The question now is what will happen to our sons.

APPENDIX

APPENDIX

Part of the French Constitution of 4 October 1958*

(*Articles 6, 8, 9, 11, 12, 13 and 15 and Titles VI, VIII, IX, XI, XII, XIII and XIV have been omitted as they are not relevant to the present work*)

PREAMBLE

The French people solemnly proclaim their attachment to the Rights of Man and to the principles of national sovereignty as defined by the Declaration of 1789, confirmed and completed by the Preamble to the Constitution of 1946.

By virtue of these principles and of that of the free determination of peoples, the Republic offers to those Overseas territories which express a desire to accept membership of the new institutions founded on the common ideal of liberty, equality and fraternity and conceived with a view to their democratic evolution.

Article 1 The Republic and those peoples of the Overseas territories who, by an act of free determination, adopt the present Constitution set up a Community.

The Community is founded upon the equality and solidarity of the peoples composing it.

---

* This translation is by William Pickles and is taken from his *French Constitution of October 4th, 1958* (Stevens, London, 1960).

193

TITLE I

Sovereignty

Article 2 France is an indivisible, secular, democratic and social Republic. It ensures the equality before the law of all citizens, without distinction of origin race or religion. It respects all beliefs.

The national emblem is the tricolour flag, blue, white and red.

The national anthem is the *Marseillaise*.

The motto of the Republic is 'Liberty, Equality, Fraternity'.

Its principle is government of the people, by the people, for the people.

Article 3 National sovereignty belongs to the people, who exercise it through their representatives and by way of referendum.

No section of the people and no individual may claim to exercise it.

The suffrage may be direct or indirect in conditions provided for by the Constitution. It is in all cases, universal, equal and secret. The right to vote, in conditions laid down by law, is enjoyed by all French nationals of either sex who are of age and in full possession of their civil and political rights.

Article 4 Parties and political groups play a part in the exercise of the right to vote. The right to form parties and their freedom of action are unrestricted. They must respect the principles of national sovereignty and of democracy.

TITLE II

The President of the Republic

Article 5 The President of the Republic endeavours to ensure respect for the Constitution. He provides, by his arbitration, for the regular functioning of the public authorities and the continuity of the State.

He is the protector of the independence of the nation, of the integrity of its territory, of respect for treaties and Community agreements.

Article 7 The President is elected at the first ballot, if an absolute majority is obtained. If this is not obtained at the first ballot, the President of the Republic is elected at the second ballot by a relative majority.

Voting begins at the time fixed by the Government.

194

The election of the new President takes place not less than twenty and not more than fifty days before the expiry of the existing President's term of office.

If, for whatever reason, the Presidency of the Republic falls vacant, or if the incapacity of the President has been certified by the Constitutional Council, at the request of the Government and by an absolute majority of its members, the functions of the President, except those conferred by articles 11 and 12 below, are performed temporarily by the President of the Senate. When a vacancy occurs, or when the incapacity is certified by the Constitutional Council to be permanent, and unless *force majeure* has been certified by the Constitutional Council, the election of a new President takes place not less than twenty and not more than fifty days after the opening of the vacancy or the declaration of the permanence of the incapacity.

Article 10 The President of the Republic promulgates laws within the fortnight following their final adoption and transmission to the Government.

Before the end of this period, he may ask Parliament to reconsider the whole law or specified articles. This reconsideration cannot be refused.

Article 14 The President of the Republic accredits Ambassadors and Envoys Extraordinary to foreign powers; foreign Ambassadors and Envoys Extraordinary are accredited to him.

Article 16 When there exists a serious and immediate threat to the institutions of the Republic, the independence of the Nation, the integrity of its territory or the fulfilment of its international obligations, and the regular functioning of the constitutional public authorities has been interrupted, the President of the Republic takes the measures required by the circumstances, after consulting officially the Prime Minister, the Presidents of the Assemblies and the Constitutional Council.

He informs the Nation of these matters by a message.

These measures must be inspired by the desire to ensure to the constitutional public authorities, with the minimum of delay, the means of fulfilling their functions. The Constitutional Council is consulted about them.

Parliaments meet as of right.

The National Assembly cannot be dissolved during the (period of) exercise of the exceptional powers.

195

Article 17 The President of the Republic has the right of pardon.

Article 18 The President of the Republic communicates with the two assemblies of Parliament by means of messages which are read for him and on which there is no debate.

If Parliament is not in session, it is specially summoned for this purpose.

Article 19 The acts of the President of the Republic other than those provided for in articles 8 (para. 1), 11, 12, 16, 18, 54, 56, and 61 are countersigned by the Prime Minister and, where necessary, by the appropriate Ministers.

TITLE III

The Government

Article 20 The Government decides and directs the policy of the nation. It has at its disposal the administration and the armed forces.

It is responsible to Parliament in the conditions and in accordance with the procedures laid down in articles 49 and 50.

Article 21 The Prime Minister is in general charge of the work of the Government. He is responsible for National Defence. He ensures the execution of laws. Except as provided for under article 13, he exercises rule-making power and appoints to civil and military posts.

He may delegate certain of his powers to the Ministers.

He deputises for the President of the Republic when necessary, as Chairman of the Councils and Committees referred to in article 15.

In exceptional circumstances he may deputise for him as Chairman of the Council of Ministers, by virtue of an explicit delegation of authority and with a specific agenda.

Article 22 The acts of the Prime Minister are countersigned, where necessary, by the Ministers responsible for their execution.

Article 23 Membership of the Government is incompatible with that of Parliament, with the representation of any trade or professional organisation on the national level, with any public employment or professional activity.

An organic law lays down the conditions in which the holders of the above offices, functions or employments are to be replaced.

196

Members of Parliament are replaced in the manner laid down in article 25.

TITLE IV

Parliament

Article 24 Parliament is composed of the National Assembly and the Senate. The Deputies of the National Assembly are elected by direct, universal suffrage.

The Senate is elected by indirect suffrage. It represents the territorial entities of the Republic, French citizens resident abroad are represented in the Senate.

Article 25 An organic law determines the length of life of each assembly, the number of its members, the payments made to them, the rules concerning qualification for and disqualification from election and the incompatibility of certain functions with membership of Parliament.

This organic law also determines the manner of the election of those who, in the event of a vacancy, replace Deputies and Senators until the next election, general or partial, to the assembly in which the vacancy occurs.

Article 26 No member of Parliament may be prosecuted, sought out, arrested, held in custody or tried on account of opinions expressed or votes cast by him in the exercise of his functions.

No member of Parliament may be prosecuted or arrested on account of any crime or misdemeanour during a parliamentary session, without the consent of the Assembly of which he is a member, except when the member is arrested in *flagrante delicto*.

Members of Parliament may be arrested when Parliament is not in session only with the authorisation of the *bureau* of the assembly of which they are members, except when the arrest is in *flagrante delicto*, when the prosecution has (already) been authorised or the final sentence pronounced.

Members are released from custody or their prosecution is suspended if the assembly of which they are members so demands.

Article 27 Any specific instruction to a member of Parliament (from an outside body) is null and void.

The member's right to vote belongs to him alone.

The (*sic*) organic law may authorise the delegation of the right to vote in exceptional circumstances. In these cases, no member may cast more than one delegated vote.

Article 28 Parliament meets as of right in two ordinary sessions per year.

The first session begins on the first Tuesday of October and ends on the third Friday of December.

The second session begins on the last Tuesday of April; it may not last more than three months.

Article 29 At the request of the Prime Minister or of the majority of the members of the National Assembly, Parliament meets in special session, with a specified agenda.

When the special session is held at the request of members of the National Assembly, the closure decree is read as soon as Parliament has completed the agenda for which it was called and at most twelve days after its meeting.

Only the Prime Minister can ask for a new session before the end of the month following the date of the closure decree.

Article 30 Except when Parliament meets as of right, special sessions are opened and closed by decree of the President of the Republic.

Article 31 Members of the Government have access to both assemblies. They are heard when they so request.

They may be assisted by Government commissioners.

Article 32 The President of the National Assembly is elected for the life of each Parliament. The President of the Senate is elected after each partial renewal.

Article 33 The sittings of both assemblies are public. A full report of debates is published in the *Journal Officiel*.

Each assembly may meet in secret session at the request of the Prime Minister or of one-tenth of its members.

198

TITLE V

Relations between Parliament and the Government

Article 34 Laws are voted by Parliament.

Laws determine the rules concerning:

civic rights and the fundamental guarantees of the public liberties of the citizen; the obligations of citizens, as regards their persons and property, for purposes of National Defence;

the nationality, status and legal capacity of persons, property in marriage, inheritance and gifts;

the definition of crimes and misdemeanours and of the penalties applicable to them; criminal procedure, amnesty, the creation of new orders of jurisdiction and the statute of the judiciary;

the basis of assessment, rate and methods of collection of taxes of all kinds; the currency system.

Laws determine also the rules concerning:

the electoral system for Parliamentary and local assemblies;

the creation of categories of public corporation;

the fundamental guarantees of civil servants and members of the armed forces;

nationalisations and the transfer of property from the public to the private sectors.

Laws determine the fundamental principles:

of the general organisation of national defence;

of the free administration of local entities, of their powers and of their resources;

of education;

of the law of property, of real-property rights and of civil and commercial contract;

of labour law, trade-union law and social security.

Finance laws determine the resources and obligations of the State, in the manner and with the reservations provided for in an organic law.

Programme-laws determine the purposes of the social and economic action of the State.

199

The provisions of the present article may be completed and more closely defined by an organic law.

Article 35 Declarations of war are authorised by Parliament.

Article 36 A state of siege is decreed in the Council of Ministers. Its prolongation beyond twelve days can be authorised only by Parliament.

Article 37 Matters other than those regulated by laws fall within the field of rule-making.

Documents in the form of laws, but dealing with matters falling within the rule-making field may be modified by decree issued after consultation with the Council of State. Such of these documents as come into existence after the coming into force of the present Constitution may be modified by decree only if the Constitutional Council has declared them to be within the rule-making sphere, by virtue of the previous paragraph.

Article 38 With a view to carrying out its programme, the Government may seek the authorisation of Parliament, for a limited period of time, to issue ordinances regulating matters normally falling within the field of law-making.

(The) ordinances are made in the Council of Ministers after consultation with the Council of State. They come into force upon publication but cease to be effective if the Bill ratifying them is not laid before Parliament by the date fixed by the enabling Act.

At the expiration of the period mentioned in paragraph 1 of this article, (the) ordinances may be modified only by law, as regards matters falling within the field of law.

Article 39 Legislative initiative is exercised by the Prime Minister and by members of Parliament.

Government Bills are considered in the Council of Ministers, after consultation with the Council of State and laid before one of the two assemblies. Finance Bills are submitted first to the National Assembly.

Article 40 Private members' Bills, resolutions and amendments which, if passed, would reduce public revenues or create or increase charges on the revenue are out of order.

200

Article 41 If, in the course of legislative procedure, it becomes apparent that a private member's proposal or amendment does not fall within the field of law-making, or is in conflict with powers delegated by virtue of article 38, the Government may demand that it be declared out of order.

In the event of disagreement between the Government and the President of the Assembly concerned, the Constitutional Council gives a ruling, at the request of either party, within a week.

Article 42 Government Bills are discussed, in the assembly to which they are first submitted, on the basis of the Government's text.

An assembly debating a Bill transmitted from the other assembly discusses it on the basis of the text transmitted to it.

Article 43 Government and private members' Bills are sent, at the request of the Government, or of the assembly then discussing them, to Commissions specially appointed for this purpose.

Bills of either type for which no such request has been made are sent to one of the permanent Commissions, the number of which is limited to six for each assembly.

Article 44 Members of Parliament and the Government have the right of amendment.

When the debate has begun, the Government may object to the discussion of any amendment which has not previously been submitted to the Commission.

If the Government so requests, the assembly concerned accepts or rejects by a single vote the whole or part of the Bill or motion under discussion, together with such amendments as have been proposed or accepted by the Government.

Article 45 Every Government or private member's Bill is discussed successively in the two assemblies with a view to agreement on identical versions.

When, as a result of disagreement between the two assemblies, a Bill has not been passed after two readings in each assembly, or, if the Government has declared the Bill urgent, after a single reading by each assembly, the Prime Minister is entitled to have the Bill sent to a joint Committee composed of equal numbers from the two assemblies, with the task of finding agreed versions of the provisions in dispute.

201

The version prepared by the joint committee may be submitted by the Government to the two assemblies for their approval. No amendment may be accepted without the agreement of the Government.

If the joint committee does not produce an agreed version, or if the version agreed is not approved as provided for in the preceding paragraph, the Government may ask the National Assembly, after one more reading by the National Assembly and by the Senate, to decide the matter. In this case, the National Assembly may adopt either the version prepared by the joint committee or the last version passed by itself, modified, if necessary, by one or any of the amendments passed by the Senate.

Article 46 Laws to which the Constitution gives the status of organic laws are passed or amended in the following conditions.

The Bill, whether Government or private members', is not debated or voted on in the first assembly in which it is introduced until a fortnight after its introduction.

The procedure of article 45 applies. Nevertheless, if the two assemblies fail to agree, the Bill may become law only if it is passed at its final reading in the National Assembly by an absolute majority of its members.

Organic laws relating to the Senate must be passed in the same terms by both assemblies.

Organic laws may be promulgated only when the Constitutional Council has certified their conformity with the Constitution.

Article 47 An organic law lays down the conditions in which Parliament votes Finance Bills.

If the National Assembly has not concluded its first reading within forty days from the introduction of the Bill, the Government sends the Bill to the Senate, which must reach a decision within a fortnight. Subsequent procedure is that provided for in article 45.

If Parliament has reached no decision within seventy days, the provisions of the Bill may be put into force by ordinance.

If the Finance Bill determining revenue and expenditure for the financial year has not been introduced in time to be promulgated before the beginning of the financial year, the Government asks Parliament, as a matter of urgency, for authorisation to levy the taxes voted and to allocate by decree the sums necessary for estimates already approved.

The time limits fixed by the present article are suspended when Parliament is not in session.

The Court of Accounts assists Parliament and the Government to supervise the application of Finance Acts.

Article 48 The agenda of the assemblies gives priority, in the order determined by the Government, to the discussion of Government Bills and private members' Bills accepted by the Government.

Priority is given at one sitting per week to the questions of members of Parliament and the replies of the Government.

Article 49 The Prime Minister, after deliberation in the Council of Ministers, pledges the responsibility of the Government before the National Assembly, on its programme or, if it be so decided, on a general declaration of policy.

The National Assembly challenges the responsibility of the Government by passing a vote of censure. A censure motion is in order only if it is signed by at least one-tenth of the members of the National Assembly. The vote may not take place until forty-eight hours after its introduction. Only votes in favour of the censure motion are counted, and the motion is carried only if it receives the votes of the majority of the members of the Assembly. If the censure motion is rejected, its signatories may not propose a further one during the same session, except in the case provided for in the next paragraph.

The Prime Minister may, after deliberation in the Council of Ministers, pledge the responsibility of the Government before the National Assembly on the passing of all or part of a Bill or motion. In this case, the Bill or part of Bill or motion is regarded as having been passed, unless a censure motion, put down within the following twenty-four hours, is passed in the conditions provided for in the previous paragraph.

The Prime Minister is entitled to seek the approval of the Senate for a general statement of policy.

Article 50 When the National Assembly passes a motion of censure or rejects the Government's programme or a general statement of Government policy, the Prime Minister must tender to the President of the Republic the resignation of the Government.

Article 51 The closure of ordinary or special sessions is automatically postponed, if need be, in order to permit the application of the provisions of article 49.

TITLE VII

The Constitutional Council

Article 56 The Constitutional Council has nine members, whose term of office lasts for nine years and is not renewable. Its members are appointed by thirds every three years. Three members are nominated by the President of the Republic, three by the President of the National Assembly, three by the President of the Senate.

In addition to the nine members provided for above, former Presidents of the Republic are *ex officio* life members of the Constitutional Council.

The President is appointed by the President of the Republic. He has a casting vote.

Article 57 The functions of a member of the Constitutional Council are incompatible with those of a Minister or member of Parliament.

Other positions incompatible with membership of the Council are listed in an organic law.

Article 58 The Constitutional Council supervises the election of the President of the Republic, with a view to ensuring its regularity.

It investigates objections and proclaims the result.

Article 59 The Constitutional Council decides, in disputed cases, on the regularity of the election of Deputies and Senators.

Article 60 The Constitutional Council supervises the conduct of referenda with a view to ensuring their regularity, and proclaims the results.

Article 61 Organic laws, before their promulgation, and the rules of procedure of the Parliamentary assemblies, before their application, must be submitted to the Constitutional Council, which pronounces in their conformity with the Constitution.

For the same purpose, (ordinary) laws may be submitted to the Constitutional Council, before their promulgation, by the President of the Republic, the Prime Minister or the President of either Assembly.

In the cases provided for in the two preceding paragraphs, the Constitutional Council decides within a month. At the request of the Government, however, if the matter is urgent, this period may be reduced to a week.

In these above-mentioned cases, reference to the Constitutional Council prolongs the period allowed for promulgation.

Article 62 A provision declared unconstitutional may not be promulgated or applied.

Decisions of the Constitutional Council are not subject to appeal. They are binding on public authorities and on all administrative and judicial authorities.

Article 63 An organic law lays down the organisation and methods of working of the Constitutional Council, the procedures to be followed in referring matters to it and in particular the time-limits within which disputes may be laid before it.

TITLE X

The Economic and Social Council

Article 69 The Economic and Social Council gives its opinion, at the request of the Government, on such Government Bills, draft ordinances, draft decrees and private members' Bills as are submitted to it.

A member of the Economic and Social Council may be appointed by the Council to appear before the parliamentary assemblies and put forward the opinion of the Council on Bills submitted to it.

Article 70 The Economic and Social Council may also be consulted by the Government on any economic or social problem concerning the Republic or the Community. Any plan or programme-Bill of economic or social character is submitted to it for its opinion.

Article 71 The composition of the Economic and Social Council and its methods of work are laid down in an organic law.